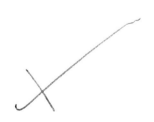

HOW
TO ENJOY
NOVELS

HOW
TO ENJOY
NOVELS

Vernon Scannell

Series Editor Melvyn Bragg

PIATKUS

© 1984 Vernon Scannell

First published in 1984 by
Judy Piatkus (Publishers) Limited of London

British Library Cataloguing in Publication Data

Scannell, Vernon
    How to enjoy novels.
    1. Fiction
    I. Title
    808.3   PN3365

    ISBN 0-86188-145-1

Designed by Zena Flax

Typeset by Phoenix Photosetting, Chatham, Kent
Printed and bound by Mackays of Chatham Ltd

contents

introduction

Most people who read books for pleasure choose to read novels. Some of the world's finest writers have expressed themselves through this form of prose fiction. And some of the trashiest productions from the most impoverished imaginations have also found a home – often lucrative – in the novel. The novel has carried the best of literature and the worst of pap. The fact that it is portable and – in paperback – comparatively cheap (free, of course, in public libraries) means that it can be moulded into the shape of anyone's day. The fact that it is – generally – the free expression of an individual view addressed directly to another individual free to pick it up or drop it at will establishes a most personal and seductive contract. There are those who argue that the novel has provided some of the very greatest works of art.

One of the daunting aspects of the novel is its range. There are marvellous novels from so many countries. Indeed, you could call them into the ring like World Champions being paraded before one of those Fights of the Century: 'From Russia, ladies and gentlemen, we give you Leo Tolstoy, Feodor Dostoevsky; from Austria, Robert Musil; from Germany, Thomas Mann;

from France, Honoré de Balzac, Gustave Flaubert, Emile Zola and Victor Hugo. . .' Over the past three centuries, a great number of countries have bred a number of great authors. For the purposes of this book, Vernon Scannell, in order to allow himself some room for perspective and substantial comment, has decided to stick to novels written in the English language.

This appears to me very sensible for several reasons. The English novel began early on and has persisted steadily: this makes it possible to trace changes and developments within a well-documented tradition. Moreover, it is not vaingloriously patriotic to point out that English literature houses some of the best novelists. Indeed, Borges – the Argentinian poet and storyteller – has gone so far as to say that 'while many countries have produced great books and great writers, only England has produced a great literature'.

Vernon Scannell concentrates, more heavily than any judicious assessment of comparative talent would warrant, on the twentieth century, as contemporary novels deal with a world which we recognize and can often more readily share in. To take a very basic point, some of the language of eighteenth and nineteenth century fiction can be off-putting. Not that you need an education to enjoy them, but it helps; and this books aims to provide the outlines and guidelines you may need.

This book transmits pleasure in the variety and inventiveness, the power and ambition to be found in novels written in English over the last 250 years. Vernon Scannell has the gift of passing on his enthusiasm, and the fair-mindedness to indicate the limitations of his preferences. In short, we get a personal history which reflects the strong opinion of one man and yet respects the full tradition about which he is writing.

There are extraordinary riches in this tradition. The novel has not only taken on the challenge of artists attempting to express their shape of the world through lengthy fictions, it has also been used to make political points, to carry religious messages, to dispute ideological concerns , to propose interpretations and meanings of life, to shock, to arouse, to bludgeon, humanize, thrill, mock, subvert; above all, perhaps, to carry the News. News from the interior of the mind, news from the territory of manners and fashions, news, quite simply, from other, often exotic, places and classes and peoples, news from everywhere, and nowhere more importantly than the individual imagination.

In his companion book on Poetry, Vernon Scannell gave a comprehensive outline of the fundamental rules of verse. Following the rules did not guarantee good verse, and breaking the rules could produce better verse, but rules there were. It is very difficult indeed to see where the rules are in novel writing. Even the most liberal and unprovocative definition – that it is a continuous prose fiction of a certain length telling a story through invented characters – is open to stricture as being too restrictive. One of the delights and strengths of novels is their infinite variety. Over-indulged speculation on 'what is a novel?', while it might be enjoyable, tends to end up in generalizations so very widely applicable that nothing much is gained by applying them; or it results in regulations which restrict and so diminish the possibilities to be found in novels.

A fairly recent danger comes from the academics. Some academics are admirable and sympathetic critics; some academics are themselves admirable novelists. Nevertheless, the teaching and programming of literature has let loose armies of 'readings' and interpretations which – whatever their quality – have threatened to divert attention from the novel itself to the theory erected around it. They can also frighten off the non-academic. Here again, Vernon Scannell's direct attack is a refreshing corrective.

Over the past twenty-five years I have read several grave and learned essays telling me about the imminent death of the novel. Movies and television and the whole global village of information were said to have robbed novels of many of their traditional functions: public story-telling, the revealing of what is new, the outward description of society, the bringing of other worlds into the mind of a reader. The novel, I was told, was to aspire to poetry for survival; it had to shed all the armoury and weaponry which made it such a force in the nineteenth century and to be content to strip itself down to a slim and naked quintessence. But no one was ever very sure what the quintessence was. It proved a slippery particle: as soon as you identified it as one kind of thing, a novel would pop up which would force you to reconsider and even rewrite the commandments.

Curiouser and curiouser, from all over the world novels began to appear which contained – although often in a differently presented form – just those characteristics thought to be banished by Modernity, and such novels then proceeded to create even further surprise by producing an impact comparable with that enjoyed by some of the Great Novels of the Past. Television and the cinema sailed on but they did not kill the novel. They co-existed with it, finding the world comfortably large enough for the three of them. And if a novel found itself 'turned into' a film or a television series, then so much the better, or so much the worse depending on the quality of the work. In neither case was the novel thereby made redundant. In my own opinion the novel is more threatened by those who seek to find any way they can to keep it exclusive and academic than by competitive or superficially traducing other media. Part of the novel's glory has been its lusty and direct connection with people and even with popularity; part of its strength has come from making its unique and individual voice listened to intently and privately outside the din of more flashy attractions.

This is not the place to present my own ideas on novels, nor would it be other than self-indulgent in this context to set off on a confessional about my own experiences as a novelist. That experience though, and those ideas, make one potentially a critical reader of such a book as this. In the event I found it thorough, stimulating, enjoyable – an excellent introduction to a mighty 'loose and baggy monster' of a subject.

Melvyn Bragg
27th April, 1984

1

WHY READ NOVELS?

There are many educated, intelligent people who do not read novels at all. They read newspapers, biographies and published diaries of figures eminent in public life, factual accounts of adventures on land, sea and in the air, of notorious crimes, of great battles fought in the remote or more recent past, books about politics, religion, philosophy, gardening, car-maintenance, life in other countries and other times, books about the stage, about music, art, architecture, science; even books about books. But when you mention novels these people will often say that they have no time for fiction. Frequently they will add that they used to read the stuff when they were young but now, with the wisdom and responsibility of maturity, they have discarded such trivial and time-wasting pursuits: the reading of fiction, they say, is a harmless pastime for those who have nothing better to do, but the serious adult should concentrate on fact, on reality, on truth. Now, if these readers are, through deficient imagination and responsiveness to language, lack of psychological curiosity and indifference to the moral bases of human conduct, unable to enjoy and learn from the reading of our major works of fiction, then they must invite sympathy; if, on the other hand, they insist that novels are a frivolous preoccupation of the immature, it must be firmly stated that they are mistaken.

Henry James, the American novelist, writing in an essay entitled *The Art of Fiction* originally published in *Longman's Magazine* in September 1884, refers to a feeling, widely spread among the reading public of the time – and, I imagine, still quite as common, except among a minority of experts, professional reviewers, professors and some practitioners – 'that a novel is a novel, as a pudding is a pudding, and that our only business with it could be to swallow it.' This popular, common-sense attitude emphasizes enjoyment, and probably many readers of fiction do indeed digest their novels in pre- cisely this way, gobbling them down without much thought, relishing the flavour and forgetting all about them until the next hunger-pang. But these readers are denying themselves the benefits and pleasures which all good novels offer, along with that of immediate entertainment, and which can provide a much deeper and lasting enjoyment. Good novels, like good puddings, are not only agreeable to swallow, they are nourishing and strengthening; they help to keep us alive. However, as with puddings, novels will do us no good unless we enjoy them, though literature may offer its readers two kinds of enjoyment, one of which is of infinitely greater value than the other.

The poet, W. H. Auden, once wrote an essay about detective stories in which he confesses that the reading of such fiction is, for him, an addiction like tobacco or alcohol. He says that, if he has some work to do, he must remove any pos- sibility of laying his hands on a detective novel because, once he has started to read one, he cannot stop until he has finished it. He observes, too, that if he happens to take up a 'who- dunnit' and finds, after reading a few pages, that he has read it before, he cannot go on with it. He is not interested in any aspect of it except the story and its outcome, and once these are known the book becomes worthless. This is because, in the majority of such tales, the characters are not living, breathing, contradictory human beings; they are pasteboard stereotypes, little more than flimsy embodiments of certain selected human attributes; the world they inhabit is equally unreal and formalized, like a stage-set. Murder is an abstract problem to be solved, not the complex, dark, pathetic or tragic and messy business it is in real life, and its solution is an intellectual exercise. In other words the detective story is fantasy, not art. In the act of reading fiction the reader will identify with one or more of the characters but, as Auden says, 'The identification of fantasy is always an attempt to avoid one's own suffering: the identification of art is a sharing in the suffering of another.'

Here then, very broadly speaking, are the two main kinds of enjoyment available to the reader of novels: we can suspend our critical faculties, our knowledge of the world and its true ways, of the infinite strangeness and ambiguities of the human heart and mind and accept unquestioningly the insubstantial, illusory world of the fantasy or romance, identifying with creatures or actions which are themselves the products of fantasy, and so escape briefly from the problems and anxieties of humdrum daily existence. On the other hand we can turn to those novels which reflect or re-create the real world in which we live, rejoice and suffer, and identify with the griefs, ambitions, ecstasies and tribulations of characters who, like ourselves and the people we know or know about, are unpredictable, self-contradictory, endlessly surprising in their conduct and destinies. The first kind of reading is almost effortless. No demands are made. The words engender images which unfold before us like a film; we are not disturbed or shocked because, if events take place which would be disturbing or shocking in real life, we are unaffected since, beneath our negative acceptance of the fiction, we know that there is no real pain involved, the people are actors or puppets, the events are not really taking place. The heroes behave heroically, the villains villainously; if the goodies are hurt or even killed we do not feel real pain or grief, only a pleasurable *frisson* of simulated emotion; when the baddies receive their just desserts our satisfaction is not impaired by the knowledge that this is not how things usually work out in actual life. The second kind of reading, the involvement with the novel as art and not as escape or fantasy, is demanding: the reader must be prepared to exercise his own imagination, his intelligence, sympathies, moral judgement and powers of concentration; the experience is challenging and, when the novel encountered is a masterpiece, it will be disturbing, even painful. The great novel may force us to question long-held assumptions about reality; we will, to some extent, be changed by it just as we would be changed by significant events in lived experience. But the pleasure from the reading will be not only far more intense than that gained from escapist fiction but it will persist long after the book has been put aside.

There is a passage in Jane Austen's *Northanger Abbey* in which a young woman is asked what she is reading. '"Oh! it is only a novel!" replies the young lady with affected indifference or momentary shame.' Then Jane Austen, asserting her authority, comments with asperity: '... only some work in which the most thorough knowledge of human nature, the happiest delineation of its varieties, the liveliest effusions of wit and humour are conveyed to the world in the best chosen language.'

The novel at its best can be all that Jane Austen claims and a great deal more. And, because it deals with largely imagined situations and characters, this does not mean that it cannot contain profound truths about humankind in relation to its society, its God or gods, the universe itself. As the distinguished contemporary author, Frederic Raphael, remarked: 'Truth may be stranger than fiction but fiction is truer.' This epigram makes a very serious point: when an author is writing directly about himself and events which have actually occurred, when all of the characters are identifiable people, he is subject to many restraints which, despite his determination to tell the absolute truth about himself and others, will inevitably impede total frankness. When we talk or write about ourselves we consciously or sub-consciously conceal or disguise those aspects of ourselves which might provoke contempt or distaste, for none of us wishes to be despised or disliked; when we speak or write of others we may reveal more of ourselves than we know, but to be completely frank about our view of other people, especially when those people are friends or enemies, is not only impossibly difficult, but may lay us open to unwelcome, even legal, reprisals. Autobiographies may supply all of the facts but even the finest tell us less than the whole truth because, in his heart of hearts, no-one wishes to have the whole truth made public; biographies tell us less than the whole truth because the whole truth cannot be known. But the novelist, whose characters possess no material existence outside the covers of the novel in which they appear, is secure from retaliation however painful the truths he may reveal about them; he can tell all because he knows all, since he is his creatures' maker. In his exploration of whatever human concerns have provoked him to write he can pierce to the heart of the matter because he has distanced himself from his characters and situations so that he can see them in their entirety.

2

WHAT
IS A
NOVEL?

Later in this book I shall be discussing in some detail a number of novels in English, but first it might be useful to ask what exactly is a novel. The word 'novel' has its origin in Latin and is related to an Italian word meaning 'a small new thing': it bears, too, a family relationship with the French 'nouvelle' or 'news'. The first English novels were in fact chronicles or stories in prose, relating events and featuring characters invented in the minds of their authors, so closely resembling real incidents and living people that they might have been extended 'news stories'. It is probably no coincidence that Daniel Defoe, who could claim to be the first English novelist – though as we shall see, he was not the first to write prose fictions – was, among many other things, a newspaperman. So the novel, in the early eighteenth century, was a 'new' literary form and it was one which gave the reader news of the world; of all forms of literature it is that which is most closely connected to lived experience. The history of Western culture can provide many examples of infant prodigies in music (Mozart, Schubert, Mendelssohn, Britten), and a number of juvenile poets and painters (Rimbaud, Chatterton, Keats,

Michaelangelo, Reynolds, Picasso) but the child prodigy as novelist is an impossibility, for the true novel must have its roots in experience of life.

The novel is, according to the Shorter Oxford English Dictionary: 'A fictitious prose narrative of considerable length, in which characters and actions representative of real life are portrayed in a plot of more or less complexity.' The 'considerable length' can be anything from three hundred thousand words to thirty thousand, though the very short novel is sometimes distinguished from the marathon event by the term 'novella'. In our own time novels may be classified under various types: among the popular lightweight works of 'escapist' fiction we have the historical or modern romance, the thriller, the whodunnit, tales of adventure, science-fiction and comedy, though each of these categories may be subdivided. For example, the thriller can include realistic stories of crime, Gothic horror tales and cloak-and-dagger spy stories, and in each of these sub-divisions the quality may vary from the level of the crudely conceived and executed to the intricately plotted, subtly observed and stylishly written. Among the more serious works of fiction we find broad categories similar to those of popular writing: historical novels, novels of action, psychological dramas, studies of human relationships, political and philosophical novels, social satire, family sagas, poetic evocations of childhood and adolescence, anatomizing of love and marriage.

In the action of a novel a segment of life is isolated from the interminable flux and attendant confusion of time: it is fixed in the framework of the novel's form and held there for our leisurely contemplation. As readers we become both observers of and, through identification, participants in the drama of the plot. I believe that we can learn more about the mysteries of human relationships, of love, hatred, jealousy, sacrifice, meanness and generosity, of the endlessly fascinating and ambiguous nature of man's aspirations and compromises, of the devices of the heart and the spirit's hunger, from reading fiction than from most other kinds of writing. The moral philosopher, the preacher or the psychologist will set down in abstract terms his notions of good and evil and try to persuade us to behave according to his convictions about what is right or salutory. The appeal is to intellect alone: our emotions – and it is from this source that most action ultimately proceeds – are rarely affected. But the novelist does not set out to persuade us to adopt his way of thinking by the use of rational argument: his words *enact* the situations of life itself: the novelist makes things happen and the reader becomes involved in those happenings. As in life our emotions are stirred by the events with which we identify ourselves. If we arrive at a moral judgement it is through feeling as much as through thinking. We are changed by the experiences we vicariously undergo and our understanding and sympathies are deepened. But to extract maximum enjoyment and profit from our reading of novels a general understanding of the way in which this literary form operates and some knowledge of its beginnings and development are desirable. For a novel is an instrument which we can use to test the sensitivity, accuracy and depth of our responses to experience and our judgements of human conduct and, like all instruments, some are more sophisticated and of better quality than others.

In this book I shall be dealing primarily with novels written in the English language. Occasionally I shall glance at the literature of other countries since English novelists have, at various times and in various ways, been influenced by foreign examples. However, I shall not attempt to deal in any detail with the great novels of Russian, French, Spanish and German literature. The novel in England and America provides a vast enough field of study and I hope to supply enough basic information and guidance about the milestones in the course of the novel to equip the reader to approach fiction with some confidence in his literary judgement and to obtain deeper pleasure from his exploration of the novels he reads.

Some of the writers and their works, especially those from the comparatively distant past, may not appeal much to modern taste, conditioned as that taste must be by the shorter, crisper fictions of our own time. For example the expansiveness and slightly archaic idiom of Samuel Richardson's novels, his tendency to adopt puritanical and, to our sceptical age, oversimplified moral attitudes, might well seem tedious to many modern readers, and the idiosyncratic style and plotless ruminations of Laurence Sterne could easily erect another kind of barrier to enjoyment. My advice to readers who are encountering the literature of the past for the first time, or after a long period of reading nothing but twentieth century fiction, is to be patient, be prepared to let your ear adjust itself to the slower, more ceremonious movement of the prose, the more leisurely establishing of scene and character; give the author – Richardson, Smollett, Sterne or whoever it may be – time to let his style and his rhythm work upon the consciousness, draw you into that remote and utterly different world. But if you find you cannot adjust yourself to the unfamiliar idiom and unsympathetic attitudes, and you are not *enjoying* the work, are even perhaps frankly bored by it, do not continue with your reading and do not, above all, feel that you personally failed through lack of sympathy, taste or sensitivity. For the fact is that much of the fiction of the eighteenth century and even some of the nineteenth offers only limited pleasure to the modern reader and is chiefly of interest to the professional critic or historian of literature.

Enjoyment, then, is the first thing we should seek in novels, remembering though that the deepest and most lasting enjoyment, that profound delight which masterpieces can give us, is often to be purchased at the price of a little hard work, a willingness to concentrate all of the faculties on the author's words, especially in the earlier pages of his novel. The rewards will be far more than commensurate with the effort expended. Few readers are temperamentally capable of equally enjoying all kinds of novels however splendid of their kind the books may be. Some of us are more easily moved by the great symphonic work like Thomas Hardy's *The Return of the Native* than by the sparkling chamber-music of Jane Austen's *Pride and Prejudice;* there are readers who prefer their novels to deal with recognizable situations and characters taken from the course of ordinary life while others prefer to read tales of high romance set in a more or less remote past, or even fantastic adventures taking place in an imagined future; some enjoy novels of violent and dramatic action while others prefer something more gentle and reflective; some have a marked taste for the dark reverberations of tragedy while others demand broad comedy or piercing satire; but whatever our preferences there is an abundance of excellent fiction in the English language to satisfy them. And I must lay stress here on the word 'excellent'.

It is true that we cannot always be reading masterpieces. The great novel, as I have said, makes its demands on our powers of concentration, imagination, emotions. We can no more live on a spiritual and intellectual diet of great richness than we can on a physical one; we will feel at times the need for plainer or lighter fare. But in turning to the lesser works of fiction there is no necessity to choose inferior stuff. The alternative to caviar and champagne is not only powdered egg and weak cocoa. There is available an almost inexhaustible stock of fiction which possesses all of the qualities of sheer readability that some badly-written commercial 'popular' tales purport to offer, yet does so without any lowering of literary standards, novels which are not only vastly entertaining but are perceptive, moving, exciting and consummately written. In the chapters which follow I hope to be able to direct my readers towards such novels as well as the great challenging works of fiction and suggest ways in which they will recognize the shoddy, third-rate imitations and be able to discard these in favour of the first-rate. In short I hope to point the way towards acquiring sound, independent literary taste.

3

WHAT MAKES A GOOD NOVEL?

With literature, as with the other arts, standards of excellence do exist. One of the oldest objections levelled at any attempt to establish criteria for judging works of art is the superficially plausible one that all assessments of the value of a book, painting or musical composition must be subjective: if the novel, picture or piece of music gives you great pleasure it is a good work of art; if it leaves you indifferent, bored or baffled it has failed in its primary purpose of transmitting enjoyment and it is therefore – as far as you are concerned – a failure, a bad work of art. If the same artistic composition gives some-one else enjoyment it is – for him – a good work of art. This objection is usually buttressed by such hoary axioms as 'beauty is in the eye of the beholder', 'one man's meat is another man's poison' or that tattered slogan of the philistine, 'I might not know much about art but I know what I like'. But it is incontrovertibly true that Dicken's *David Copperfield* is a better novel than, say, James Hilton's *Goodbye, Mr Chips* or that Emily Brontë's *Wuthering Heights* towers dwarfingly above any romantic fantasy by Ruby M. Ayres or Barbara Cartland, and that the superiority of those two great novels to their inferiors can be clearly demonstrated.

language

language
What distinguishes the good novel from the less good, or plain bad, is first the quality of the writing. The major novelist uses language with that almost obsessive regard for each word's rightness – its meaning, associations, sound, colour and texture – that the best poets display. And this scrupulous searching for the absolutely right words reflects his equally scrupulous resolve not to falsify the emotions that he is delineating and exploring. He is concerned, first and foremost, with truth.

plot

plot
The next quality which marks the first-rate novel is the way in which the story unfolds, the novelist's structuring of the events which constitute the 'plot'. As E. M. Forster, in *Aspects of the Novel,* puts it: a *story* is '. . .a narrative of events ranged in their time-sequence.' The *plot* of a novel is something more complex. It is '. . .a narrative of events, the emphasis falling on causality.' In it, incidents do not simply recur, one after the other, but are interrelated: the effects of something which has happened quite early in the narrative may not manifest themselves until much later. The plot can be used by its author to demonstrate a particular view of life, its essential irony, the power or weakness of erotic love, the hollowness of material success, the indomitability of the human spirit over adversity, and so on. A well-constructed plot will give the reader surprises, but these must be legitimate surprises caused by events which can be seen, on reflection, to be logically and emotionally the inevitable outcome of prior events; it will serve as a means of demonstrating facets of the personalities and temperaments of the novel's characters, and the novel which does not contain convincing, solid, living characters must be counted a failure.

character

character
Fictional characters can be convincingly drawn through the ways in which they behave in the various incidents of the plot,

but there are, of course, other methods available for the persuasive portrayal of character. Physical description, while it can be a help, is perhaps the least important and some writers are at pains to avoid providing precise details of the appearance of their characters, believing that it is more effective to allow the reader's imagination to supply them. It is enough, generally, for the author to let us know in outline which important physical characteristics his creatures possess and even this does not have to be done by direct description. For example, references to certain dominant features could be made in dialogue by one of the other characters in the story, and it is through direct speech that so much of character can be conveyed, qualities such as wit and intelligence, stupidity and insensitivity, imagination or its lack. Dialogue can also, of course, tell us a lot about a speaker's class, education or regional origins, and the author's uses of it can provide one criterion for the judgement of a novel's merit.

character

dialogue

Skilfully written conversation must sound like natural speech and its forms should be not merely appropriate to the speaker's class, generation and psychological type but an important index to other, more individual attributes. It must sound in the mind's ear like ordinary talk but it is not an actual transcription of common speech. Dialogue mimes the rhythms, vocabulary and syntactical patterns of conversation but it does not reproduce them. Modern novelists very rarely imitate colloquial speech by the use of phonetic spelling, for they long ago discovered that this device, even when used by someone with a sharp ear for verbal idiosyncrasies, is almost always miserably ineffective. Take this example from Somerset Maugham's first novel, *Liza of Lambeth* (1897). Liza, an eighteen-year-old cockney girl, joins a group of men and women who are dancing in the street to the music of an organ-grinder:

dialogue

> When she came to the group round the barrel-organ, one of the girls cried out to her:
>> 'Is that yer new dress, Liza?'

23

dialogue

'Well, it don't look like my old one, do it?' said Liza.

'Where did yer git it?' asked another friend, rather enviously.

'Picked it up in the street, of course,' scornfully answered Liza.

'I believe it's the same one as I saw in the pawn-broker's dahn the road,' said one of the men to tease her.

'Thet's it; but wot was you doin' in there? Pledgin' yer shirt, or was it yer trousers?'

'Yah, I wouldn't git a second-'and dress at a pawn-broker's!'

'Garn!' said Liza indignantly. 'I'll swipe yer over the snitch if yer talk ter me. I got the mayterials in the West Hend, didn't I? And I 'ad it mide up by my Court Dressmiker, so you jolly well dry up, old jelly-belly.'

'Garn!' was the reply.

Liza had been so intent on her new dress and the comment it was exciting that she had not noticed the organ.

The reader already knows that the characters in this scene are all cockneys so he will hear the pronunciations of the idiom without any prompting from those clumsy visual aids which, in fact, are not aids at all since, taken simply as phonetics, they are remarkably inaccurate. There is, too, something unpleasantly patronizing about those deliberate mis-spellings. When Maugham records the speech of the educated middle classes in his other writings he employs orthodox spelling but the talk of the lower orders is always set down in this 'comical' music-hall language. Try reading the above passage aloud and you will see how uncomfortably the words leave the lips and fall upon the ear. And I am sure you will notice how the public-school educated, middle-class author mixes up his idioms and has the sub-literate cockney girl suddenly speaking in the tones, and employing the usages, of prep-school badinage: '. . .so you jolly well dry up, old jelly-belly.'

Another distressing weakness in this short passage is the recurring habit of unnecessarily qualifying almost every statement made by the actors – '. . .rather enviously', '. . .scornfully answered Liza', '. . .to tease her', '. . .said Liza indignantly'. None of those adverbs or phrases is serving any useful purpose at all since the sense of what has been said has already made plain the feelings of envy, scorn, mockery and so on. A look at the use of dialogue by a contemporary writer, Paul Bailey, in his novel *Trespasses* (1970) will show how an accurate ear for cadence, syntax and idiom can reproduce the effects of idiosyncratic speech (in this case that of the South London, lower middle class, rather seedy mother of the narrator's landlady) without recourse to clumsy phonetic spelling or adverbial explanation:

> I was already on the stairs when Mrs Goacher – in her doorway, with a pink glow behind her – called out 'Do you drink, Mr Hicks?'
> 'Yes.'
> 'Would your poison happen to be gin?'
> 'Sometimes, yes.'
> 'Care to join me for a tipple then? I haven't got designs on you; you'll be quite safe. The truth is, I'm feeling a bit on the lonely side tonight, wanting company. Madam has left her poor old mother alone with the bottle – actually, dear, she doesn't know I've got one – and I've been sat here watching bloody television, hoping for someone nice like you to come in. So get down them stairs this minute.'
> A single lamp, shaded pastel pink, lit the room.
> 'There should be time for two doubles apiece before the cow gets back.'
> 'Who's the cow?'
> 'Who else? My bloody daughter, bloody Ruby. Mrs Dinsdale to you.'
> 'Oh.'
> I looked at the painting above the mantelpiece: an Oriental woman with a green face.
> 'She bought me that. That's the only reason it's on the wall, I can tell you. I think she bought it out of spite, because she knew it would clash with everything else in the room. I like rosy colours, always did. "Rosy means cosy" was my mother's motto, and it goes for me too. So what does my kind, thoughtful daughter buy me for Christmas, Mr Hicks? That monstrosity. The word *is* monstrosity, isn't it?'
> 'Yes. Why?'
> 'I ask because Ruby's for ever correcting me over

dialogue

the way I speak. She says I disgrace her.'

'Oh no.'

'Oh yes, dear. Oh yes. She's a terrible snob, Ruby is. You'd think her shit was scented soap, the way she carries on. Why are you standing?'

'There's a cat in the chair.'

'Push him off.' She clapped her hands. 'Off you go, Timmy sweetheart. Brush the fur off before you sit down, dear. That's something else she did to me. Well, not to me exactly, to *him*: that helpless little animal there. Had him attended to. "I don't want him passing water" – just like her, saying that; she'd never say a plain word for a plain deed – "I don't want him passing water on my landings, making the place smell nasty." "It's nature," I said to her. "You can't go against nature." "It's either that", she said, "or having him put down. Make your choice." Well, I couldn't spend the rest of my life with his death on my conscience, could I? Imagine yourself in my shoes for a minute – I mean, which evil would you have chosen? I *have* a heart, Mr Hicks: there's enough pain in the world without me adding to it, even to the putting-down of a cat. So Ruby won again, as she usually does. It hurts me, you know, when I think about it: cutting off a dumb creature's knackers just to please the whim of a house-proud bitch like my Ruby. I say she's house-proud, which she is, but the funny thing about it is that she has all the pride and I do all the work. That's life, as they say. Here's tonic for your gin, dear, if you want it. I take a little hot water with mine, like my old mother used to do.'

Then, leaning over me, her hand on my arm, she asked in a whisper 'Has she been up to your room yet?'

If you read Mrs Goacher's monologue aloud you will find that her voice, realistically and with all its mannerisms, asserts its individuality with an authenticity which is almost uncanny.

You may think that the comparison I have made between Maugham, writing at the turn of the century, and Bailey in and about comparatively recent times is an unfair one, but if we go further back, to 1850, when *David Copperfield* was first published in book-form (it had previously been serialized) we shall find that a writer of Dicken's quality, in his handling of direct speech, shows none of the **dialogue** snobbish, maladroit inaccuracy of Maugham, and his occasional use of phonetic spelling is unobtrusive:

> After we had jogged on for some little time, I asked the carrier if he was going all the way?
>
> 'All the way where?' inquired the carrier.
>
> 'There,' I said.
>
> 'Where's there?' inquired the carrier.
>
> 'Near London,' I said.
>
> 'Why, that horse,' said the carrier, jerking the rein to point him out, 'would be deader than pork afore he got over half the ground.'
>
> 'Are you only going to Yarmouth, then?' I asked.
>
> 'That's about it,' said the carrier. 'And there I shall take you to the stage-cutch, and the stage-cutch that'll take you to – wherever it is.'
>
> As this was a great deal for the carrier (whose name was Mr Barkis) to say – he being, as I observed in a former chapter, of a phlegmatic temperament, and not at all conversational – I offered him a cake as a mark of attention, which he ate at one gulp, exactly like an elephant, and which made no more impression on his big face than it would have done on an elephant's.
>
> 'Did *she* make 'em, now?' said Mr Barkis, always leaning forward, in his slouching way, on the footboard of the cart with an arm on each knee.
>
> 'Peggotty, do you mean, sir?'
>
> 'Ah!' said Mr Barkis. 'Her.'
>
> 'Yes. She makes all our pastry and does all our cooking.'
>
> 'Do she though?' said Mr Barkis.
>
> He made up his mouth as if to whistle, but he didn't whistle. He sat looking at the horse's ears, as if he saw something new there; and sat so for a considerable time. By-and-by, he said:
>
> 'No sweethearts, I b'lieve?'
>
> 'Sweetmeats did you say, Mr Barkis?' For I thought he wanted something else to eat, and had pointedly alluded to that description of refreshment.
>
> 'Hearts,' said Mr Barkis. 'Sweethearts; no person walks with her?'
>
> 'With Peggotty?'
>
> 'Ah!' he said. 'Her.'
>
> 'Oh, no. She never had a sweetheart.'

dialogue

'Didn't she, though?' said Mr Barkis.

Again he made up his mouth to whistle, and again he didn't whistle, but sat looking at the horse's ears.

'So she makes,' said Mr Barkis, after a long interval of reflection, 'all the apple parsties, and does all the cooking, do she?'

I replied that such was the fact.

'Well. I'll tell you what,' said Mr Barkis. 'P'raps you might be writin' to her?'

'I shall certainly write to her,' I rejoined.

'Ah!' he said, slowly turning his eyes towards me. 'Well! If you was writin' to her, p'raps you'd recollect to say that Barkis was willin'; would you?'

'That Barkis was willing,' I repeated, innocently. 'Is that all the message?'

'Ye-es,' he said, considering. 'Ye-es. Barkis is willin'.'

In both the extracts from *Trespasses* and *David Copperfield* the dialogue advances the plot and tells us something about the characters of the speakers; we are listening to the self-revealing talk of real people. The language of Liza is that of a Victorian *Punch* cartoon-caption and she remains a cut-out figure, a flimsily constructed puppet.

atmosphere

atmosphere

Liza of Lambeth will also serve as a negative example of the next quality which we demand of the novel, and that is the creation of atmosphere, the sense of place, of external reality, including physical action and sensation. Here are the first two paragraphs of Chapter One:

It was the first Saturday afternoon in August; it had been broiling hot all day, with a cloudless sky, and the sun had been beating down on the houses, so that the top rooms were like ovens; but now with the approach of evening it was cooler, and everyone in Vere Street was out of doors.

Vere Street, Lambeth, is a short, straight street leading out of the Westminster Bridge Road; it has forty houses on one side and forty houses on the other, and these eighty houses are very much more like one

another than ever peas are like peas, or young ladies
like young ladies. They are newish, three-storied
buildings of dingy grey brick with slate roofs, and they
are perfectly flat, without a bow-window or even a
projecting cornice or window-sill to break the straight-
ness of the line from one end of the street to the other.

This description gives us the requisite information: it is a hot
Saturday in August and the scene is a street in Lambeth. But the
evocation of heat and lassitude, the physical immediacy of the
place and time, are as perfunctorily sketched as the language is
undistinguished. We encounter tired adjectives and verbal
linkings in the very first sentence: 'broiling hot', 'cloudless sky',
'like ovens'. A little later we are told that the houses are more like
one another 'than ever peas are like peas; or young ladies like
young ladies'. This double simile is particularly ill-conceived.
The reference to peas of course reminds us instantly of the cliché
'as like as peas in a pod'; the second comparison is simply
unfocused, blurring rather than illuminating the objects being
described (the houses), for the implication that young ladies
resemble each other as closely as peas is ludicrously false.

clichés

The use by any author of clichés is a sure sign of inferior writing.
The word *cliché* derives from the French, meaning a stereotype
plate, a photographic negative or a cast or mould, and our use of
it denotes the stereotype phrase, that word or conjunction of
words which has become dull, frayed and lifeless through
over-use. Clichés are to be avoided not only because they signify
laziness or unoriginality in the writer but because they are either
too obvious to be of value or completely inaccurate. 'He turned
as white as a sheet', for instance, is, apart from being
stereotyped, quite false, even if we accept that all sheets are
white; 'dead as a doornail' tells us nothing about the look of a
corpse and 'raining cats and dogs' not only fails to present the
phenomenon it purports to depict, it actually obscures it.
Furthermore verbal clichés are always found with those deeper
faults in a writer, clichés of observation and response. When the

clichés   language is fresh, vigorously alive, you can be sure that the
author's insights and discoveries will be of value.

Let us now look at the opening two paragraphs of
another novel, Ernest Hemingway's *A Farewell to Arms*
(1929):

> In the late summer of that year we lived in a house in a
> village that looked across the river and the plain to the
> mountains. In the bed of the river there were pebbles
> and boulders, dry and white in the sun, and the water
> was clear and swiftly moving and blue in the chan-
> nels. Troops went by the house and down the road and
> the dust they raised powdered the leaves of the trees.
> The trunks of the trees too were dusty and the leaves
> fell early that year and we saw the troops marching
> along the road and the dust rising and leaves, stirred
> by the breeze, falling and the soldiers marching and
> afterwards the road bare and white except for the
> leaves.
>
> The plain was rich with crops; there were many
> orchards of fruit trees and beyond the plain the moun-
> tains were brown and bare. There was fighting in the
> mountains and at night we could see the flashes from
> the artillery. In the dark it was like summer lightning,
> but the nights were cool and there was not the feeling
> of a storm coming.

This is masterly scene-setting and the prose carries, beneath
its apparent simplicity, marvellously evocative under-
currents. The language is as direct as it could be, every word
is quite plain, mainly of Anglo-Saxon derivation; there are no
attempts to dramatize through the use of rich verbal orches-
tration. But those carefully placed repetitions of 'house',
·'river', 'dust', 'trees' and 'leaves' work with the deliberate,
marching pace of the sentences almost hypnotically on the
reader's senses. And Hemingway is doing more than creating
a convincing background and sense of place: the word 'falling', which overtly describes the leaves, is placed close to
soldiers', adumbrating their future fate, and running through
the passage is a sense of impending violence which prepares
the reader for the novel's main theme, war, its bitterness
and waste.

imagery and symbolism

The brief remarks made above might sound closer to the language of poetic criticism than commentary on prose fiction, and it is true that the best novelists frequently use descriptions of the weather or landscape as images or symbols which prepare the reader for the novel's principal themes and key events. The sea in *Moby Dick* (1851) by Herman Melville is splendidly described in realistic terms, but it is also a symbol for the dark deep mysteries, the ebb and flow, the dangers and sustenances of human existence; the two contrasting houses, the remote, tempest-ravaged Heights and the sheltered, peaceful Grange in Emily Brontë's *Wuthering Heights* (1847) are presences or metaphors for the opposing strains in Catherine Earnshaw's nature; the alarmingly convincing evocation of the marshes at the beginning of *Great Expectations* (1861) and the terrifying appearance of the convict; the variations played on the theme of the sea in *Dombey and Son* (1847) are all symbols as well as accurately observed physical realities, and that superb account of Sergeant Troy's exhibition of his skill with the sword in Thomas Hardy's *Far From the Madding Crowd* (1847) is packed with dramatic and psychological significance:

**imagery
and
symbolism**

> He flourished the sword by way of introduction number two, and the next thing of which she was conscious was that the point and blade of the sword were darting with a gleam towards her left side, just above her hip; then of their reappearance on her right side, emerging as it were from between her ribs, having apparently passed through her body. The third item of consciousness was that of seeing the same sword, perfectly clean and free from blood held vertically in Troy's hand (in the position technically called 'recover swords'). All was as quick as electricity. . .
>
> In an instant the atmosphere was transformed to Bathsheba's eyes. Beams of light caught from the low sun's rays, above, around, in front of her, well-nigh shut out earth and heaven – all emitted in the marvellous evolutions of Troy's reflecting blade, which seemed everywhere at once, and yet nowhere

specially. These circling gleams were accompanied by a keen rush that was almost a whistling – also springing from all sides of her at once. In short, she was enclosed in a firmament of light, and of sharp hisses, resembling a sky-full of meteors close at hand.

We do not need a Freud to tell us that the sword is a phallic symbol and that this scene prefigures the inevitable surrender of Bathsheba to the gallant soldier.

The qualities, then, that distinguish the novel of true literary merit from the inferior work of fiction are, first, the prose-style, the way in which the author uses language with precision, an ear for its harmonies and rhythmic possibilities, the avoidance of commonplace phrasing and cliché; next, the solidity and psychological accuracy of the characterization and the organization of the events which constitute the plot; finally, the authenticity of the dialogue and the way in which it is used to highlight characteristics of the actors, to establish their reality and to forward the action of the plot, and the way that, in description of objects, landscape and seasons, poetic imagery or metaphor can add to the power and richness of the entire work. None of these elements of the novel is separable from the others, with the possible exception of the plot. In other words it is impossible for an ill-written novel to contain convincing and memorable characters or a haunting sense of place; if the dialogue is clumsily handled the writer is not likely to use the language of description or reflection with any greater skill. But we do find some novels which contain good plots, that is to say accounts of events and actions so organized that they keep the reader in suspense and he feels that he must read on simply to find out what happens in the end, yet the writing may be undistinguished and the psychological insight nugatory.

plot vs character

Plots of this kind do not, as the plots of most good novels do, grow out of the interrelation of the characters, their psychological needs and responses to experience, their moral decisions and actions; these plots are prefabricated, worked out intellectually, and then the characters – or puppets – are fitted into their roles and the action is played out. Many commercially successful novels have been constructed in this way and, in fact, most modern best-sellers are of this kind and they are very often turned into films, sometimes into very good films. This type of novel often appeals to film-makers more than serious and finely achieved works of fiction and, indeed, it is more likely to lend itself to movie adaptation. From time to time films based on great or at least seriously conceived works of fiction have been made, often with disastrous results. Very occasionally a good novel has been adapted for the screen successfully, that is to say an enjoyable movie has been made featuring characters and situations taken from the book, but always the transference has been reductive. The films of *Great Expectations, Tess of the D'Urbervilles, Moby Dick, Sons and Lovers,* however well photographed, directed, cast and acted, could never provide more than a thin and superficial substitute for the experience of reading the works upon which they are based.

**plot
vs
character**

Popular novels which are carefully plotted, full of accurate circumstantial detail, reflecting contemporary desires, dreams and fantasies, or dramatizing obsessive fears, nightmares and anxieties, will appeal to the studios not *despite* the flimsiness of characterization and perfunctoriness of the writing but *because* of these weaknesses. The film-maker is provided with a satisfactory story which he can use as a framework and, by the careful casting of good actors and actresses, the employment of gifted writers to supply crisp and believable dialogue, experienced and talented cameramen and the exercise of his own directorial gifts, he can inject vigorous life into what was formerly insubstantial fantasy, useful only to the undiscriminating reader for painlessly passing a few leisure hours. The novel whose appeal is entirely dependent on its plot, in which the quality of the writing is thin and colourless, the presentation of character, setting and dialogue based, not on a close and perceptive observation of real life, but on the stereotypes of other mechanical fiction, is similar to the poem which provides stock emotional responses to experience in unimaginative verse-patterns: it is the doggerel of prose.

entertainment

I hope that what I have so far said has not given my reader the impression that I minimize the value of pure entertainment in the novel. On the contrary I am convinced that the novel which does not offer an enthralling narrative of some kind is unlikely to find its place among the finest examples of prose-fiction. The narrative may be an externalized one of physical action or it may be a drama enacted within the consciousness of one or more of the characters in the book; it could deal with the conflict of nations, of individuals or of ideas. One of the most exciting and rewarding novels published in recent years is a very short work of less than a hundred pages by the Ulster writer, Brian Moore, with the remarkably unresonant title of *Catholics* (1972). It is set in the very near future when the ecumenical movement in the Christian Churches has resulted in the Church of Rome rationalizing much of its dogma and rituals, abandoning the mystical bases of its doctrines and concerning itself with strengthening its purely ethical and political authority. But one little monastery on a small island off the Irish coast has held out against all change and, as a result, has become a kind of shrine, a last refuge of the ancient holiness, to which pilgrims come hungry for the old mysteries and consolations that their faith once offered. The new Vatican resolves that this monastery must be suppressed and sends a plenipotentiary, a young American revolutionary priest, to persuade the old Irish Abbot and his monks of their folly in persisting in the discredited forms of worship and adhering to the obsolete miraculous beliefs. The confrontation of the old world and the new forms the substance of the book.

A brief and, of course, only partial summary of the kind I have given would, I am sure, persuade most readers that they would rather read a month-old local newspaper than anything so dull as *Catholics*. But, through the beauty and economy of the writing, the subtle and perceptive explorations of character, the dramatic juxtapositions of temperaments and ideas, the evocation of place and the brilliantly accurate dialogue, the novel is continuously witty, absorbing, deeply moving and enjoyable.

discrimination

The more fiction of high quality that we read the more discerning our judgement will become and the greater our impatience with and distaste for the ill-made, mediocre, unoriginal and superficial. Literary critics and other commentators on the cultural scene have, for some years, been prophesying the death of the novel as a serious literary form, but, despite the rival narrative media of film and television and the claims upon the reader's attention of books of factual reportage, the novel remains obstinately and vigorously alive, though some of the forms it now takes may show little obvious resemblance to its predecessors of two or three centuries ago. Some knowledge of those earlier forms is a great help to anyone who wishes to read novels with discrimination and to extract maximum pleasure and profit from his reading. So, in the pages that follow, I shall attempt to provide an outline of the development of the novel in the English Language from its infancy to its by no means enfeebled present state.

4

THE EVOLUTION OF THE NOVEL

the beginnings

The novel is the baby of the main established literary forms in the English language. The ancestry of English poetry can be traced back at least 1300 years to Caedmon, the inspired monk and former herdsman who, entirely without learning, versified passages from the Scriptures, and to the anonymous *Beowulf*, the first great poem to be written in any modern language (Anglo-Saxon). English drama clearly derives from the medieval Miracle Plays of the late thirteenth or early fourteenth century but most literary historians agree that the novel, as a distinctly identifiable form, did not appear until the second decade of the eighteenth century with Daniel Defoe's *Robinson Crusoe* (1719). This does not mean that no sustained stories in prose had been written before that time.

Sir Thomas Malory's *Morte d'Arthur*, printed by Caxton in 1485, is the first great imaginative prose work in English, though it is obviously not a novel but a translation from the French and other sources of some of the Arthurian legends, its main themes being the quest of the Holy Grail and the chief events of Arthur's reign, culminating with the dissolution of the Round Table. John Lyly (1554–1606) wrote a prose 'romance' in two parts, the first *Euphues: the Anatomy of Wit* published in 1578 and the second, *Euphues and his England* in 1580, but his work holds little of interest for anyone except specialists in the literature of the period though it might be worth mentioning that his strange, highly rhetorical and ornate style has given the word 'Euphuism' to our language – not to be confused with 'euphemism' which has a quite different meaning. The story in Lyly's work is the most slender of pegs on which to hang his reflections on love, the inconstancy of women, the folly of youth and, in the second part, his celebrations of Queen Elizabeth and the glories of her realm. Sir Philip Sidney's *Arcadia* (1590) though sometimes spoken of as an 'Elizabethan novel' is in fact a prose pastoral romance, having absolutely none of that concern with real people in real life that the true novel always displays: it is a long, and to most readers, I would guess, unreadably boring melange of nymphs and shepherds from classical literature, and knights, kings and princesses from medieval romance.

The nearest thing to a novel that any Elizabethan produced is Thomas Nashe's *The Unfortunate Traveller, or The Life of Jacke Wilton* (1594) and it could reasonably be called the first picaresque romance in English. 'Picaresque' is a term deriving from a Spanish word 'picaro' meaning 'a rogue', so picaresque stories are tales dealing with the exploits of rogues and scoundrels, the first examples of these being written in Spanish. Nashe's prose is about as different from Sidney's as could be imagined and *The Unfortunate Traveller* can still be read today for the vitality and colour of the language. But it cannot properly be labelled a novel: it is a sequence of frequently improbable adventures taking place during the reign of Henry VIII in which the 'hero', Jacke Wilton, becomes a page to the Earl of Surrey, whom he accompanies to Italy where they encounter Erasmus and Sir Thomas More and other historical personages. Wilton assumes the identity of the Earl and runs away with an Italian courtesan. After leaving the service of the Earl, Wilton survives an outbreak of the plague in Rome and he witnesses many scenes of violence, torture and bloodshed, finally repenting his shiftless ways and marrying the courtesan.

the Noble Savage and *The Pilgrim's Progress*

In 1678 were published two imaginative prose works of start-ling dissimilarity in content and execution yet both of which can be seen as important to the development of English prose fiction: one was Mrs Aphra Behn's *Oroonoko, or The History of the Royal Slave* and the other was John Bunyan's *The Pilgrim's Progress.* It was believed that Aphra Behn had spent most of her childhood in Surinam, Guiana, returning to England at the age of eighteen and marrying a city merchant, though more recent research suggests that her foreign sojourn was an invention. She became a successful playwright but *Oroonoko* is the work for which she is best known today. In this curious book we see the first appearance in literature of the idea of the Noble Savage, for her hero, Oroonoko, the grandson of an African King, is handsome, brave and – implausibly enough – well-read in European literature.

Aphra Behn's story is not quite the kind of thing we would expect to read in a traditional novel. The story is a romance, improbable, essentially operatic, and the characters are theatrical puppets rather than recognizable people. But it is a remarkable piece of fiction and it does show, for the first time, that a work of imaginative prose can be something more than a fanciful and trifling tale, that serious ideas can be intro-duced into the texture of a story, for *Oroonoko* could legiti-mately be claimed as the first anti-imperialist, anti-slavery polemic presented as fiction.

The Pilgrim's Progress, too, though generally recog-nized as a masterpiece of our literature, is not a novel, though it possesses some of the ingredients of the new form: lively dialogue and characterization and a strong narrative drive. But Bunyan's purpose in writing it was homiletic: he is a preacher propounding Christian truths in the form of allegory, though this allegory does resemble the pattern of the picares-que novel with, instead of a rogue, an upright religious man on a journey which takes him among all types of people and circumstance towards the goal of spiritual salvation. It is a work unique in literature and the universality of its appeal may be judged by the fact that it has been translated into well over a hundred languages and dialects.

Robinson Crusoe – the first novel?

Almost half a century later, with the publication of *Robinson Crusoe*, we encounter the first English prose fiction which might fairly be called a novel. Daniel Defoe (1660–1731), its author, is one of the most extraordinary men in the history of English literature. He was born in London, the son of James Foe, a butcher, and he changed his name to Defoe at about the time of his first imprisonment in 1703 when he was fined, pilloried and jailed for six months for writing a pamphlet, *The Shortest Way with the Dissenters,* which satirically attacked the prevailing religious intolerance of the period. After his release he started his newspaper, *The Review* in 1704, worked as a secret agent and, probably, a double-agent, and was prosecuted by the Whigs for publishing anti-Jacobite pamphlets, again suffering brief imprisonment. As a younger man he had taken part in Monmouth's rebellion and subsequently joined William III's army.

This gifted man, largely self-educated and fluent in half a dozen languages, did not write the book for which he is best known until he was fifty-nine years of age. *Robinson Crusoe*'s claim to be the first proper English novel can be seen as a kind of accident for Defoe, in this book, did not set out deliberately to produce a work of fiction but to deceive his readers that the account of Crusoe's various adventures, including the central one of his long sojourn on the island, was a true story, a work, not of imagination but of autobiography. Its source seems to have been the accounts written of an actual castaway's experiences, Alexander Selkirk who, in 1703, sailed for Brazil and was marooned on the island of Juan Fernandez for over four years. What makes the book something other than a kind of literary forgery, a fake autobiography, makes it, in fact, a novel is Defoe's tremendous skill in creating the character of Crusoe. Until the publication of this book the characters in prose fiction, from the nymphs and shepherds of the Elizabethan pastoral romances to the Noble Savage of Aphra Behn's *Oroonoko* – and including the figures in *The Pilgrim's Progress* which, however brilliantly realized, remain embodiments of isolated human virtues and failings – are two-dimensional, lacking the breathing

substance, the quirky self-contradictoriness, the unpredicta-
bility of living human beings.

Crusoe convinces us of his reality partly because
Defoe takes minute pains to persuade us of the reality of
everything else in the book, even the smallest and least significant of details. Furthermore Crusoe is never so resourceful as
to strain credulity: he shows the weaknesses and limitations
that persuade us of his actuality. When he first goes to sea he
is for some time troubled by sea-sickness and when, in the
early part of the book, before he is cast away on the island,
and he is captured and taken into slavery by Barbary corsairs,
the treatment he receives is undramatically mild. His escape is
no prodigy of heroism, and when he is wrecked his good
fortune in surviving is made convincing by the careful
accumulation of circumstantial detail. The account of his
repeated journeys to the wrecked ship to salvage all that
would be of use to him is retailed with absolute authenticity
and, on the final trip before the wreck is broken up and
dispersed by another storm, he finds some money and his
response to and reflection upon this discovery is a brilliantly
economical piece of character delineation:

> I had been now thirteen days on shore, and had
> been eleven times on board the ship; in which time I
> had brought away all that one pair of hands could well
> be supposed capable to bring, though I believe verily,
> had the calm weather held, I should have brought
> away the whole ship piece by piece. But preparing the
> twelfth time to go on board, I found the wind begin to
> rise. However, at low water I went on board, and
> though I thought I had rummaged the cabin so effect-
> ually as that nothing more could be found, yet I
> discovered a locker with drawers in it, in one of which
> I found two or three razors, and one pair of large
> scissors, with some ten or a dozen of good knives and
> forks; in another, I found about thirty-six pounds value
> in money, some European coin, some Brazil, some
> pieces of eight, some gold, some silver.
> I smiled to myself at the sight of this money. "O
> drug!" said I aloud, "What art thou good for? Thou art
> not worth to me, no, not the taking off of the ground;
> one of those knives is worth all this heap. I have no

manner of use for thee; even remain where thou art, and go to the bottom as a creature whose life is not worth saving." However, upon second thoughts, I took it away; and wrapping all this in a piece of canvas, I began to think of making another raft; . . .

*Robinson
Crusoe –
the first
novel?*

Moll Flanders – the rogue as a woman

Defoe was an immensely prolific writer – a full list of his published works contains over 250 titles – but students of the English novel will be concerned only with *Robinson Crusoe, Moll Flanders* (1722), *A Journal of the Plague Year* (1722) and *Roxana* (1724). Of the last three *Moll Flanders* is the one which today can be read with probably the most enjoyment. Like *Robinson Crusoe* it is written in the first person and it shows a similar gift for conveying facets of personality through the careful selection and observation of physical detail; it is also, like his most famous work, a novel masquerading as autobiography.

**Moll Flanders –
the rogue
as a woman**

Moll's mother was convicted for petty theft but, since she was pregnant, her sentence of transportation was delayed until she had been delivered of her child, the heroine of Defoe's story:

> My mother was convicted of felony for a petty theft, scarce worth naming, viz. borrowing three pieces of fine holland of a certain draper in Cheapside. The circumstances are too long to repeat, and I have heard them related so many ways, that I can scarce tell which is the right account.
>
> However it was, they all agree in this, that my mother pleaded her belly, and being found quick with child, she was respited for about seven months; after which she was called down, as they term it, to her former judgment, but obtained the favour afterward of being transported to the plantations, and left me about half a year old, and in bad hands you may be sure.

The 'bad hands' belonged, it appears, to a band of gypsies but Moll escapes from these or is deserted by them – she, as

**Moll Flanders –
the rogue
as a woman**
narrator cannot be sure since the event occurred so long ago –
and is looked after by a kind of foster mother until she is old
enough to go into service. She is fortunate in her employers
who are kind and, for the period, surprisingly liberal, and
since they have two daughters of a similar age to Moll she is
allowed to share their lessons, so she acquires a reasonable
education. But there are also two older sons, the eldest of
whom seduces her, but this probable disaster is turned to good
fortune when the younger proposes marriage and is finally
accepted. Moll, however, remains in love with the older
brother and it is a measure of Defoe's gift in characterization
that he can persuade us of her duplicity and toughness yet, at
the same time, communicate her charm. When her husband
dies after only five years of marriage Moll writes:

> I confess I was not suitably affected with the loss of
> my husband; nor can I say that I ever loved him as I
> ought to have done, or was suitable to the good usage
> I had from him, for he was a tender, kind, good-
> humoured man as any woman could desire; but his
> brother being so always in my sight, at least while we
> were in the country, was a continual snare to me; and I
> never was in bed with my husband, but I wished
> myself in the arms of his brother. And though his
> brother never offered me the least kindness that way
> after our marriage, but carried it just as a brother
> ought to do, yet it was impossible for me to do so to
> him; in short, I committed adultery and incest with
> him every day in my desires, which, without doubt,
> was as effectually criminal.

In the meantime the elder brother has married someone else
so Moll, as a reasonably affluent and attractive widow, is
determined to make a second prudent marriage. As she says:
'I had been tricked once by that cheat called love, but the
game was over; I was resolved now to be married or nothing,
and to be well married or not at all.' But when she does marry,
to a linen-draper, he turns out to be wildly extravagant and
irresponsible and the marriage ends with his fleeing,
bankrupt, to France.

Next Moll marries a sea captain and sails with him to Virginia where she discovers he is her own half-brother; she returns to England, lives in Bath and becomes the mistress of a rich man who later repents and dismisses her. She is then deceived into marriage by a highwayman posing as a rich gentleman and when the two fortune-hunters discover the truth about each other they separate, she to contract yet another marriage to a respectable bank-clerk. When he dies she becomes a thief and is imprisoned in Newgate where she meets the highwayman again. She is sentenced to death but reprieved and transported back to Virginia. Finally she and the former highwayman, both completely reformed and penitent, return to England to end their days together.

So *Moll Flanders* is, in fact, a picaresque novel but with the rogue as a woman, and it is a considerable imaginative achievement. It is also a work which explores the effects of environmental forces on character, showing not only how Moll becomes the person she is but the reasons why.

**Moll Flanders –
the rogue
as a woman**

Gulliver's Travels

The only other book of the period which might lay claim to being classified as a novel is *Gulliver's Travels* (1726) but, despite Swift's impressive narrative powers, the fantastical setting and the satirical intentions of the work disqualify it as a true representative of the new form. Satire can, of course, be the principal intention of a proper novel but it must be executed through the behaviour of real people in recognizably real situations. The motivating force behind *Gulliver's Travels* is Swift's disgust with human folly and pretension; the ideas are embodied in grotesques, in the six-inch high Lilliputians, the gigantic Brobdingnagians, the horse-like Houyhnhnms and the disgusting Yahoos. Robinson Crusoe and Moll Flanders are fully realized humans who live in the imagination just as later the major characters of Dickens convince us of their physical and spiritual reality; the novelist may be moved by hatred and disgust at the spectacle of human evil and stupidity but he cannot allow himself to be

*Gulliver's
Travels*

obsessed by it. He must see things steadily and see them whole and, in the last analysis, if he lacks charity, lacks love, he will never present the World with justice.

the eighteenth century

Both *Robinson Crusoe* and *Moll Flanders,* then, may be read with enjoyment by modern readers but the book which literary historians would name as the next important work to extend the development of the new literary form is almost intolerably prolix and tedious to twentieth-century tastes. However, in even such a brief survey of the English novel as this, it would be absurd to omit any reference to it, and the circumstances of its composition are in themselves of interest. The book is *Pamela* and it was written by Samuel Richardson (1689–1761) and published in four volumes during 1740 and 1741.

Pamela

Richardson was the son of a joiner and received only a rudimentary formal education. At the age of seventeen he was sent from his home in Derbyshire to London, where he was apprenticed to a printer. He worked hard and successfully, marrying his employer's daughter, setting up his own business, first in Fleet Street and then in Salisbury Court, London. He had, from an early age, been a prolific correspondent, not only on his own behalf but as a scribe for people less skilful with the pen, and when he was in his very early teens he would write love-letters for young women in the neighbourhood. Knowing of his enthusiasm for and practice in the epistolary arts two friends, who were also printers, asked him to write 'a little volume of letters', in a common style, on such subjects as might be of use to country readers who are unable to indice for themselves' and it was from this exercise that *Pamela* arose, so one of the earliest and certainly one of the most influential of English novels was composed almost by accident.

One of the class of letters that he was commissioned to write was intended to instruct 'handsome girls who were obliged to go out to service, as we phrase it, how to avoid the snares that might be laid against their virtue'. In the writing of these letters Richardson remembered a story he had once heard of a young girl who, at the age of twelve, was taken into the service of a wealthy family and there she resisted all temptations, 'improving daily in beauty, modesty and genteel and good behaviour' and finally married her employer's son, behaving 'with so much dignity, sweetness and humility, that she made herself beloved of everybody, and even by his relations, who at first despised; and now had the blessings both of rich and poor, and the love of her husband'. The recollection of this tale fired Richardson, who was a devout moralist, with the ambition to write, in the form of letters written by the girl to her parents, a story 'in an easy, natural manner . . . to promote the cause of religion and virtue'. The title page of *Pamela* reads as follows:

Pamela

> Pamela: or Virtue Rewarded. In a Series of Familiar
> Letters from a beautiful young Damsel to her Parents.
> Now first published in order to cultivate the Principles
> of Virtue and Religion in The Minds of the Youth of
> both Sexes. A Narrative which has its Foundation in
> Truth and Nature; and at the same time that it agree-
> ably entertains, by a Variety of curious and affecting
> Incidents, is intirely divested of all those Images,
> which, in too many Pieces calculated for Amusement
> only, tend to inflame the Minds they should instruct.

Pamela was an instant and resounding success. Texts from it were preached by clergymen from their pulpits; its author received innumerable letters from admiring and delighted ladies, and Alexander Pope – that least sentimental or puritanical of poets – asserted that it 'would do more good than many volumes of sermons'. In his scheme for writing *Pamela*, Richardson, despite his utterly sincere resolve to produce a work which would be morally uplifting and instructive, had hit upon a recipe for a best-seller which is still effectively used by popular novelists of our own time: this is the plot of suspended seduction. Will the heroine succumb or not, or will her

Pamela   seducer, who is referred to throughout Richardson's narrative as Mr B., abandon his pursuit or be forced to accept her terms of nothing less than holy matrimony? And in spite of the book's enormous length – certainly excessive by later standards – Richardson does manage to keep the suspense going.

The morality of *Pamela* which was so warmly endorsed by so many readers, seems in the eyes of the twentieth century to be very dubious indeed. Pamela herself is priggish, egotistical and calculating and when Mr B. is at last reduced to proposing marriage her joy is self-righteous and takes no account at all of the fact that his pursuit of her has been a sequence of contemptuous belittlement. Indeed, by no means everyone at the time was uncritical of the book. A number of parodies were published ridiculing Richardson's novel, and one of these, by far the best, was Henry Fielding's *Joseph Andrews*.

Henry Fielding

Henry
Fielding

Fielding (1707–1754) was an entirely different type of man and of writer from Richardson. He was of superior social class, educated at Eton and Leyden University in the Netherlands where he studied Law, leaving at the age of twenty-one to live by his wits and pen in London. He wrote plays, with a few small successes but at least as many failures, and later returned to his legal studies and was called to the Bar in 1740. He was an agreeable, high-spirited man with a very lively sense of humour and little patience with hypocrisy, sentimentality and moral complacency, so *Pamela* presented a tempting target for good-natured satire. In *Joseph Andrews* (1742), Joseph is drawn as Pamela's brother and, like his virtuous sister, he is a servant who is subjected to similar temptations to those so admirably overcome by his sister. One of the principal characters, perhaps the most splendidly realized of them all, is Parson Adams, who is, with his small vanities, absent-minded simplicity, kindness and powerful innocence one of the most memorable and endearing creations in English literature. He is based on Don Quixote and his journey on the road to London with Joseph, who has been sacked from his footman's job for resisting the sexual overtures of Lady Booby and Mrs Slipslop, follows a Quixotic sequence of improbable and farcial adventures.

In one scene of broad comedy the narcissistic and profligate Beau Didapper invades Mrs Slipslop's bedchamber in mistake for that of Joseph's sweetheart, Fanny, and Parson Adams, hearing a scream, rushes to protect maiden virtue and in the darkness of the room he is misled by the feel of Didapper's smooth skin and Mrs Slipslop's beard into believing the latter to be the assailant to whom he administers a severe drubbing. This kind of levity enraged Richardson who referred to *Joseph Andrews* as 'a lewd and ungenerous engraftment' on the pure stem of *Pamela*.

Joseph Andrews was a modest success but it did not rival the immense popularity of *Pamela*. However it set Fielding on his course as a novelist and he went on to produce a satire on the misguided popular adulation accorded to public figures in *The History of the Life of the Late Mr Jonathan Wild the Great* (1743) and then his masterpiece, *The History of Tom Jones* (1749). *Tom Jones,* of all the eighteenth-century novels, can be read today with the most enjoyment. The hero is a fictional prototype which anticipates the 'anti-hero' of many English novels of the twentieth century for Tom, though personable, courageous and essentially good-hearted, is also easily seduced from the path of virtue and his principles are often discarded under pressure from his senses or for reasons of expediency. The novel contains a wealth of sharply observed characters, a wonderful sense of vitality and sheer love of life and his portrayal of women, though doubtfully acceptable to the modern feminist, is always sympathetic and often tender.

Smollett

Tobias Smollett (1721–1771) whose first novel, *Roderick Random,* was published the year before *Tom Jones,* lacked Fielding's gift for delineating character with both objectivity and compassion. Smollett was more of a caricaturist than a full-scale portraitist and he was deficient, too, in Fielding's ability to

Smollett   organize his material into a coherent and satisfying unity, yet he must be mentioned here if only for the influence he exercised on the work of Charles Dickens and because he is the first English novelist to write about life at sea. *Roderick Random* calls upon a good deal of Smollett's own experience, for its author was, like the eponymous hero, a Scot who went to sea as surgeon's mate and took part in the British Navy's attack on Cartagena. But the book is emphatically not an autobiographical novel: it is an often funny, occasionally bizarre picaresque fiction, written in a sinewy, undecorated prose.

Smollett's last, and many critics say his best, novel is *The Expedition of Humphry Clinker* (1771) which is written in the form of letters penned by a country squire, Matthew Bramble, various of his relations and the doubtfully literate but vigorously articulate lady's maid, Winifred Jenkins, describing the adventures encountered by the family party as it travels through England and Scotland. Humphry Clinker is a disreputable ostler whom the family adopt as postilion and who turns out to be a man of surprising talents and resources. There are three love stories in the narrative, all of which are concluded to the satisfaction of the people concerned, but these are of less interest than the episodic adventures in Bath, London, Harrogate and Edinburgh which take place against a vividly realized background of those places in the later eighteenth century.

The epistolary novel is probably an extinct literary form but in his use of it Smollett extends the possibilities of the later novel's range by showing how a particular event can seem to change its nature as it is presented through the eyes of different characters. In other words *Humphry Clinker* marks an important stage in the development and sophistication of the novel and we shall see how rapidly this progress accelerates in the nineteenth century when prose fiction comes into its exciting and robust early maturity. But before leaving the eighteenth century we must first glance at one of the strangest works of imaginative prose in our language, *The Life and Opinions of Tristram Shandy* by Laurence Sterne, which was originally published in parts, the first two volumes appearing in 1760, four in 1761, a further two in 1765 and the final volume in 1767.

Tristram Shandy

Sterne was the son of a professional soldier and, though his schooling suffered in consequence, he was able to make his way to Cambridge University where he was a sizar to Jesus College (he performed certain menial duties in exchange for tuition) and obtained a Master's degree. He was ordained and became Vicar of Sutton-in-the-Forest in 1738, married in 1741 but caused some scandal and a lot of domestic distress by his attentions to other ladies. When he moved to London he achieved some literary and social success but the appearance of the four volumes of *Tristram Shandy* brought upon him opprobrious comment from influential men of letters including Dr Johnson, Samuel Richardson, Horace Walpole and Oliver Goldsmith, all of whom were puzzled by the manner and morally outraged by the matter of this strange new work. And it is easy, even now, to sympathize with their perplexity if not their indignation.

Tristram Shandy is a novel in that it is a work of prose which sets out to create an imaginary world inhabited by recognizable human beings, but when compared with the solid reconstructions of reality, the strict sequentiality of Fielding and Smollett, it seems almost crazily fragmented and confused. We have to wait until Book Three before the hero is born, and the narrative is constantly interrupted by apparently irrelevant digressions, disconnected episodes, unresolved sentences, weird manipulations of language and syntax and startling admixtures of the bawdy, farcical and sentimental. What Sterne is doing here is something extraordinarily 'modern': he is anticipating in his own inimitable manner the methods and intentions of certain major novelists – whose work we shall later be examining – writers like Virginia Woolf, James Joyce and William Faulkner who, in their different ways, have attempted to show events taking place within the protagonists' consciousness, the world within the skull. *Tristram Shandy* is almost surrealistically exploring a kind of reality new in prose fiction, the reality of the mind's behaviour. Sterne exposes the fallacy that our processes of thought and feeling are orderly, consequential and under our control by using language to imitate the twists, convolutions

*Tristram
Shandy*

and leaps, the darkness and brilliance, the absurd, pathetic and comic nature of our interior lives. His work will not appeal to every taste: there are at least as many readers who find him infuriating, or just plain unreadable, as there are those who regard him as a source of infinite delight.

the early nineteenth century

the early
nineteenth
century

The literary historians' divisions of their subject into categories, movements and centuries are notoriously difficult to justify but they must be accepted simply as convenient ways of setting out a very broad outline of the immensely complex and involuted processes of change and development. Obviously, there was no moment at which writers became self-consciously aware that they were no longer exploring, without guidelines or much confidence, the possibilities of the new form of the English novel and that they were now working securely in a medium as firmly established as, say, lyric poetry, the blank verse epic or prose drama. Fanny Burney published her three novels *Evelina*, *Cecilia* and *Camilla* between 1778 and 1796 yet she outlived Jane Austen by more than two decades, dying in 1840 at the unusually advanced age of eighty-eight. Mrs Radcliffe, whose 'gothic' romance, *The Mysteries of Udolpho* (1794) gave much pleasure to the young Jane Austen, who wrote an affectionate parody of the genre in *Northanger Abbey*, also outlived the younger author, dying in 1823. Dates of births and deaths can be confusing, just as rigid attempts at classification may mislead, yet, nevertheless, the novel, in the delicate hands of Jane Austen, did achieve a kind of consummation after which its claim to be taken just as seriously as the other great literary forms became an unquestioned fact.

Jane Austen

Jane Austen

Jane Austen (1775–1817) was born at Steventon in Hampshire, the daughter of the Rector, and she led a life of genteel and spinsterish provincialism at her birthplace and later at

Bath, Southampton, and Winchester, where she spent her last **Jane Austen**
days and where she is buried. She received one proposal of
marriage which she accepted but, the very next day, turned
down. This lively, intelligent and quite attractive young
woman would be unremarkable except that she published six
novels, all of which not only occupy an unassailably important
position in the history of our literature but may be read today
with as much pleasure as when they were first written.

She is not a novelist who appeals to all tastes. Her contemporary, Sir Walter Scott (1771–1832), wrote this in his
diary, nine years after her death:

> Read again for the third time at least, Miss Austen's
> finely written novel of *Pride and Prejudice.* That
> young lady had a talent for describing the involve-
> ments and feelings and characters of ordinary life
> which is to me the most wonderful I ever met with.
> The big Bow-Wow strain I can do myself like any now
> going; but the exquisite touch which renders ordinary
> common-place things and characters interesting from
> the truth of the description and the sentiment, is
> denied to me. What a pity such a gifted creature died
> so early!

But Charlotte Brontë (1816–1855), a few years later, after the
publication of her own romantic and tempestuous *Jane Eyre,*
set down a quite different view of *Pride and Prejudice:*

> . . .an accurate, daguerreotyped portrait of a common-
> place face! a carefully fenced, highly cultivated
> garden, with neat borders and delicate flowers; but no
> glance of a bright, vivid physiognomy, no open
> country, no fresh air, no blue hill, no bonny beck. I
> should hardly like to live with her ladies and
> gentlemen in their elegant but confined houses.

These contrasting reactions to Jane Austen's work represent
the duality of critical response that has persisted until the
present. One reader will find her witty, perceptive and
capable of penetrating to permanent truths about human
relationships through the scrupulous observation of
commonplace events and conduct; another will regard her as

51

anaemic, over-preoccupied with trivial matters and undistinguished people. But if a taste for the grand scale, the symphonic, precludes a capacity to take delight in the exquisite though quieter effects of the chamber-work, then it is the auditor and not the artist who will be the loser. What concerns us here is that, however each of us may react to her work, none can deny that she brought to the novel a concern with structure, an ability to create a small world and populate that world with completely convincing people whose every word and action contribute to the sympathetic reader's understanding of life's ironies and consolations.

Her most popular novel, though not necessarily her finest, has always been *Pride and Prejudice* (1813) and one can see why the circle of characters – Mrs Bennet, the mother obsessed with match-making; Collins, the sycophantic and opportunist clergyman; the delightful and clever Elizabeth, whose Pride is set against the snobbish Prejudice of Darcy, the aristocrat whose hauteur conceals a warm heart – continue to exert their appeal. Although they belong firmly in their time and place they are, paradoxically, representatives of permanent human attributes and we can recognize their types and circumstances in the very different context of late twentieth-century life.

Sir Walter Scott – the regional novelist

Sir Walter Scott who, as we have seen, was so generously appreciative of Jane Austen's qualities as a novelist could not have been more different in his own aims and achievements. He was the first great historical novelist and, perhaps more important, the first great *regional* novelist, for it is only those works with a Scottish background that retain their power to grip the imagination. Scott had achieved both great popular recognition and a considerable fortune as a poet with *The Lay of the Last Minstrel, Marmion, The Lady of the Lake, Rokeby* and other vigorous narrative poems, but by 1814 his popularity had been eclipsed by Lord Byron and it was then he turned to fiction and produced, anonymously, his first novel, *Waverley*. It was an immediate triumph and Scott set about producing its numerous successors with prodigious invention and stamina. Some of these works possess admirable qualities: *The Heart of Midlothian*, for example, offers a fine gallery of both major and minor characters and incidents of dramatic action which still come to exciting life, and *The Antiquary* is a fine romantic novel of intrigue, love and high adventure which was, as the author himself maintained, chief favourite among all his novels. The character of the Antiquary is drawn with great skill and sympathy and, though it is, according to Scott, based on a boyhood friend it is generally recognized that it is, to a large extent, a self-portrait.

**Sir
Walter Scott –
the regional
novelist**

E. M. Forster, in his *Aspects of the Novel,* admits candidly that he does not care for Scott because he '. . .is seen to have a trivial mind and a heavy style'. But Forster concedes that 'he could tell a story. He had the primitive power of keeping the reader in suspense and playing on his curiosity'. There is some justice in Forster's observations but his view is that of a professional novelist and one who is deeply concerned with the technical problems of style and structure. Scott's command of form was slight and he failed signally to add anything to the narrative methods of his predecessors. But he did produce work which delighted a large public and in doing so he helped greatly to encourage Scottish authors and publishers to produce an indigenous regional fiction. Susan Ferrier (1782–1854), John Galt (1779–1839) and Michael Scott (1789–1835) all brought out readable novels but it was James Hogg, 'the Ettrick shepherd' (1770–1835) who wrote what must surely be one of the most remarkable novels of the first half of the nineteenth century and, indeed a work which not only keeps much of its haunting power but has increased its intensity for even the most sophisticated readers of the present time. This was *The Private Memoirs and Confessions of a Justified Sinner* published in 1824.

The novel was probably conceived by Hogg as a satire on the extreme forms of religious fanaticism that stemmed from the teachings of the sixteenth-century Swiss reformer, John Calvin, and flourished in Scotland with particular vigour and often with miserable consequences. The justified sinner of Hogg's novel is Robert Wringhim who, convinced that he is one of God's elect believes that he is therefore freed from the restraints imposed by moral law on ordinary folk and, acting as 'the scourge of God' he can with impunity destroy all whom he considers to be deserving of punishment. He is encouraged in his beliefs, or madness, by a mysterious young man who is at first seductively sympathetic but gradually comes to dominate him utterly and drives him to self-destruction. The young man is the embodiment of pure evil or, literally the devil incarnate. The book today reads less as a satire than a dark allegory of the power of evil and it is entirely original in construction and style.

the Victorians

For those readers who wish to follow a serious course of study in the English novel it would be necessary to make at least a brief acquaintance with the brilliant satires of Thomas Love Peacock (1785–1866) and the accomplished political novels of Benjamin Disraeli (1804–1881) but for our purpose here of tracing only the principal stages of the novel's evolution it would seem expedient to spend a little more time examining that great promontory in the history of fiction, the work of Charles Dickens.

Charles Dickens

Dickens is surely the most famous novelist in English literature and his fame, unlike that of, say, Chaucer, is accompanied by a real knowledge of his writings though in recent years this knowledge tends to be derived from a vicarious experience of the originals through the media of the musical adaptation, television and cinema rather than from a reading of the novels. That the books lend themselves readily to such adaptations is undeniable but the fact that these comparatively superficial translations should result in a neglect of the printed works is to be regretted, for Dickens, master of narrative, characterization and dialogue was above all a great *writer* and when we are deprived of the words he actually wrote, when the superbly realized verbal images are, however sensitively, translated into two-dimensional pictures on the screen, or his exquisitely cadenced and accurate passages of direct speech are re-hashed as cross-talk or music-hall song, what is forfeited is precisely that which makes him a great artist.

Charles Dickens (1812–1870) was the son of John Dickens, a clerk in a Navy Pay Office, a cheerful, improvident and incorrigibly optimistic man on whom the character of Mr Micawber in *David Copperfield* was almost certainly based. This novel, often referred to as 'autobiographical', was in the strict historical sense only tenuously so. The fictional David Copperfield was an orphan whose childhood was spent at Blunderstone near Yarmouth whereas Dickens was born at Landport, a suburb of Portsea, from which the family moved in 1816 to Chatham, so the novelist's earliest memories were not of the flats of Yarmouth, which he did not see until 1849, but of the very different landscape of Kent. However, the novel is autobiographical in the sense that it could not have been written had not Dickens experienced the crisis of his father's imprisonment for debt and his own appalling stint, at the age of eleven, working in the blacking factory in London.

Dickens was largely self-educated and his earliest serious reading, as recorded in John Forster's great biography, was the fiction of Smollett, Fielding, Defoe and *Don Quixote* and the influence of the picaresque tradition can be clearly seen in his early *Posthumous Papers of the Pickwick Club*, published originally in twenty monthly instalments beginning in April, 1836 when the author was twenty-four, especially in the relationship between Sam Weller and Pickwick, the comic, earthy and sceptical servant and the idealistic, unworldly master encountering an assortment of rogues and human oddities on their various adventures. But the comic picaresque element in Dicken's fiction is only a small strand in the sumptuous fabric of the entire output. His next work, *Oliver Twist*, is ostensibly an exposure of the inhumanity of the contemporary workings of the poor law, but, with all of its apprentice faults, it is a powerful allegory of the opposition of good and evil. The chief flaws are prolixity and the cumbersome irony of the satire, but in the creation of the vicious characters, Sikes and Fagin, he shows formidable power in the evocation and embodiment of wickedness.

A common criticism of Dickens is that his characters, whether comic or villainous, are caricatures, grotesque exaggerations of reality, but this objection seems to be based on a misunderstanding of the nature of his genius. He is not a realistic novelist in the manner of his French contemporary Gustave Flaubert (1821–1880) or of later English novelists like H. G. Wells and Arnold Bennett; his representation of people is essentially poetic and dramatic; the reality he communicates is the piercing reality of poetic vision, the object seen as if for the first time, stripped of the obscuring veils of long association, preconception and familiarity. He does not confirm our customary notions of what people are like: he reveals them to us as they really are. This is why we have all encountered in our daily lives people who remind us or seem to be reincarnations of Dickens's characters. Mr Micawber, Uriah Heep, Wackford Squeers, Mr Pecksmith, Thomas Gradgrind, Dolly Varden, Mrs Gamp, possess their massive breathing actuality in the pages of the fictions but the replicas of them that we meet in quotidian life, while they may be smaller and their main features less obtrusive, are essentially and recognizably the same people.

Dickens is a poet, too, in his deployment of imagery and symbolism. In the early pages of *David Copperfield* the sea at Yarmouth is shown as the giver of life (Mr Peggoty is a fisherman and his home is a converted upturned boat) yet the destroyer also (Ham is drowned in attempting to rescue the evil Steerforth) and in *Dombey and Son* it makes its appearance at key-moments as physical reality and emblem of death and resurrection. In this novel the development of steam railway, which was to change the face of industrial and commercial Britain, is effectively introduced as both symbol and concrete fact: it symbolizes the inexorable progress of technological advancement, the increase, for the privileged few, of wealth and the potential destructiveness of the machine. Ironically, the ruthless and acquisitive Carker, who is the agent of Dombey's ruin, is killed by a train.

Here are two very brief extracts from *Dombey and Son* which may serve as examples or reminders of Dickens's emotional and dramatic range. In the first, from the opening chapter, he is describing the death of Mrs Dombey whose

little daughter, Florence, has been brought to the bedside to
be held in her mother's embrace, and the image of the sea,
used metaphorically, is brought into the novel for the first time
like the partial, hinted whisper of a musical subject which will
be later elaborated and resolved in the symphonic whole:

**Charles
Dickens**

> The two medical attendants exchanged a look
> across the bed; and the Physician, stooping down,
> whispered in the child's ear. Not having understood
> the purport of his whisper, the little creature turned
> her perfectly colourless face, and deep dark eyes
> towards him; but without loosening her hold in the
> least.
> The whisper was repeated.
> 'Mama!' said the child.
> The little voice, familiar and dearly loved,
> awakened some show of consciousness, even at that
> ebb. For a moment, the closed eyelids trembled, and
> the nostril quivered, and the faintest shadow of a smile
> was seen.
> 'Mama!' cried the child sobbing aloud. 'Oh dear
> Mama! oh dear Mama!'
> The Doctor gently brushed the scattered ringlets of
> the child aside from the face and mouth of the mother.
> Alas how calm they lay there; how little breath there
> was to stir them!
> Thus, clinging fast to that slight spar within her
> arms, the mother drifted out upon the dark and
> unknown sea that rolls round all the world.

And next the description of Carker's violent death on the railway track which concludes the powerful account of his
unavailing flight from retribution:

> He paid the money for his journey to the country-
> place he had thought of; and was walking to and fro,
> alone, looking along the lines of iron, across the valley
> in one direction, and towards a dark bridge near at
> hand in the other; when, turning in his walk, where it
> was bounded by one end of the wooden stage on
> which he paced up and down, he saw the man from
> whom he had fled, emerging from the door by which
> he himself had entered there. And their eyes met.

**Charles
Dickens**

In the quick unsteadiness of the surprise, he
staggered, and slipped on to the road below him. But
recovering his feet immediately, he stepped back a
pace or two upon that road, to interpose some wider
space between them, and looked at his pursuer,
breathing short and quick.

He heard a shout – another – saw the face change
from its vindictive passion to a faint sickness and
terror – felt the earth tremble – knew in a moment that
the rush was come – uttered a shriek – looked round –
saw the red eyes, bleared and dim, in the daylight,
close upon him – was beaten down, caught up, and
whirled away upon a jagged mill, that spun him round
and round, and struck him limb from limb, and licked
his stream of life up with its fiery heat, and cast his
mutilated fragments in the air.

When the traveller, who had been recognized,
recovered from a swoon, he saw them bringing from a
distance something covered, that lay heavy and still,
upon a board, between four men, and saw that others
drove some dogs away that sniffed upon the road, and
soaked his blood up, with a train of ashes.

Vanity Fair –a novel without a hero

**Vanity Fair –
a novel
without
a hero**

Of all the novelists mentioned so far Dickens must be the most
enjoyable for modern readers and his achievement, so
towering and comprehensive, influenced all of his immediate
successors and continues to exert its influence on many
writers of our own time. His near contemporary, William
Makepeace Thackeray (1811–1863) inevitably suffers by
comparison but his first and best novel, *Vanity Fair*, still offers
considerable pleasure today. Thackeray's social position and
education were quite different from those of Dickens. He was
born in Calcutta but was sent to England when he was six or
seven years old where he attended prep school followed by
Charterhouse and Trinity College, Cambridge. He became a
journalist, was a regular contributor to *Punch* and editor of the
Cornhill Magazine, not attempting a novel until he was in his
mid-thirties.

The sub-title of *Vanity Fair* is 'A Novel without a Hero'

and in this book Thackeray is consciously aiming at creating a *Vanity Fair –* work of fiction which realistically presents a picture of English **a novel** morals and manners at a given time through the actions of a **a hero** disparate but interrelated set of characters revolving round the careers of two contrasted females, Becky Sharp, an intelligent but utterly unscrupulous daughter of a poor artist and a French dancer, and Amelia Sedley, a pretty but stupid rich girl. The plot is fairly complicated and Thackeray presents a host of well-observed characters who make their exits and their entrances, but one senses a kind of moral or spiritual lacuna at the novel's centre. The most interesting characters, Becky herself, Sir Pitt Crawley and George Osborne are amoral, if not totally immoral, and the virtue attributed to Captain Dobbin and Amelia seems a concomitant of their lack of intelligence and imagination.

Thackeray's other novels show little in the way of development in construction, characterization or vision. *Pendennis* (1848–50), which is his most clearly autobiographical novel, has splendid scenes in the earlier chapters, especially the accounts of Penn's experiences at Oxford, but the work is often digressive though there are a number of neatly sketched minor characters such as the genial rogue, Captain Strong, the outrageous Lady Clavering and Morgan, Major Pendennis's blackmailing servant. *Henry Esmond* (1852), highly regarded by some critics, is a historical novel set in the eighteenth century and the reconstruction of the period of Queen Anne is done with great skill. The characters, however, do not, for me, come fully to life and, while the complications of the plot are deftly manipulated, the work as a whole lacks that vital spark of imaginative passion which animates the best fiction.

the Brontës

Imaginative passion is a quality which no-one would deny to **the Brontës** the work of Emily and Charlotte Brontë – the writings of the third sister, Anne, are of far slighter stature and it is doubtful her books would be known today except for the association with her eminent siblings and the potency of the Brontë legend. Emily's *Wuthering Heights* (1847) is indisputably one of the finest novels in the language. In outline the story seems melodramatic: Heathcliff is a gypsy child who has been rescued from the streets of Liverpool by Mr Earnshaw and brought back to Wuthering Heights to be reared as one of his own children. After Mr Earnshaw's death his son, Hindley, jealous and resentful of Heathcliff, bullies and humiliates the foundling, who has fallen in love with Catherine Earnshaw, Hindley's sister. Heathcliff overhears Catherine say that she would consider marriage to himself a degradation, and in rage and despair he leaves the house, returning three years later, having made money, to find that Catherine is married to the decent but rather insipid Edgar Linton. He then sets about avenging himself on both the Earnshaws and the Lintons and in the process destroys not only his beloved Catherine and the unfortunate Isabella Linton but, finally, himself.

That the young Emily Brontë, starved of human society except that of her sisters and brother, isolated in the bleak Haworth vicarage, should produce a great romantic novel is surprising enough, but more amazing still is that its form is not only handled with the greatest skill and assurance but that it also looks forward to techniques that were not to be employed again for another fifty years or so. The opening sequences are recounted by Mr Lockwood, the stranger from the South who has rented Thrushcross Grange from Heathcliff and who has no part in the main drama which, at the time of his arrival on the scene, is already drawing to its close. He becomes fascinated by the strange situation prevailing at Wuthering Heights and encourages Nelly Dean, the servant, to tell him of the events which have led to the present wretched and mysterious situation. Adroitly Emily Brontë weaves into Nelly's story first-person narrations by Isabella and Catherine Linton and the heart of the tragic tale is revealed. Then Lockwood leaves the district, returning a few months later to find a quite different and happier atmosphere at Wuthering Heights, and Nelly is able to supply the end of the tale.

This sophisticated method of unfolding the story is not, of course, an exercise in originality for its own sake. Beginning the novel at a moment when much of the action of

the plot, including the death of the heroine, has already the Brontës
occurred is a subtly effective way of forestalling the reader's
possible resistance to the improbability of the tale. These
things, unlikely though they may seem, have already
happened. Furthermore, the introduction of Mr Lockwood,
the passive onlooker and auditor, is an invitation for us to
identify with him and it is an invitation which is impossible to
refuse. We, the readers, are drawn to and fascinated by the
mystery just as he is.

We cannot leave *Wuthering Heights* without a mention of what is tantamount to an inanimate but never absent
character in the narrative: the presence of the landscape of
the West Riding moors in all weathers and moods. The sense
of place broods over and through this novel in a way that is
unequalled until we come to the Wessex novels of Thomas
Hardy yet, with Emily Brontë, it is extremely difficult to pin
down precisely the way in which she creates this atmosphere.
There are no set passages of description but the reader's
awareness of the natural background never weakens: placed
throughout the novel are echoes of the sound of the beck in
the valley, of lashing rain, the wind; there are small sharp
images of the time of harvest, hazel and stunted oak, the moor
sheep, the glens and hills, snow and frost, summer flowers.

Emily's sister Charlotte is best known for her novel
Jane Eyre (1847) and its great popularity is understandable.
The earlier scenes of the orphaned Jane at Lowood Asylum,
where she suffers miserably as a child though less so, later, as
a teacher, are poignantly evoked. When she leaves there to
become Governess at Thornfield Hall to Mr Rochester's
small ward and falls in love with her grim master, the
improbabilities of the plot begin to strain credulity. Rochester
is captivated by Jane's wit and indomitable spirit and
proposes marriage but the wedding does not take place for
she discovers the presence of Rochester's lunatic wife who is
kept locked away in an attic. Jane runs away and, after almost
perishing on the moors, she is rescued by a clergyman, the
Reverend St John Rivers and his sisters. She has almost
arrived at a decision to marry the cleric when she receives a
mysterious telepathic message from Rochester, whom she still
loves. She hurries back to Thornfield Hall and discovers that it

has been burnt down and that Rochester, in a doomed attempt to rescue his mad wife, has been crippled and blinded. Finding him wretched and humbled she marries him; his sight is partly restored and they discover happiness together.

The principal events are difficult enough to swallow and there are other incidental scenes – such as the unequivocally masculine Rochester disguising himself as a female gypsy fortune-teller to discover the secrets of Jane's heart – which do not help the suspension of disbelief, yet the sheer drive of narrative energy, Charlotte Brontë's own passionate conviction in the authenticity of the feelings she is portraying, go a long way towards compelling assent. The reader must make similar allowances to those which must be made for the enjoyment of a romantic opera. The circumstances may be preposterous but the anguish and ecstasy are real.

Charlotte's *Villette* (1853) is a re-working of *The Professor,* an earlier novel which had been rejected by the publishers, and – unlike *Jane Eyre* – it is firmly based on her own experience of two years of teacher-training in Brussels. It is a more accomplished work than *Jane Eyre* and the element of fantasy wish-fulfilment, so strong in her first novel, is subtly merged with shrewdly observed realities of character and environment. Lucy Snowe, the heroine, takes a teaching job in a girls' school in Brussels where she meets John Bretton, an English doctor whom she had known in childhood, but though she is attracted by him her deeper feelings are engaged by M. Paul, the superficially less appealing professor who conceals beneath his acerbic and domineering front a warm and sympathetic nature. The ending of the story, with M. Paul going off to the West Indies and leaving Lucy in charge of her own little school, is deliberately and admirably ambiguous. He may return to marry her, as they both hope, or he may have perished in the violent storms which are active at the time of his return voyage.

Trollope

Trollope   In the novels of the Brontë sisters, and especially in *Wuthering Heights,* we find something like an apotheosis of the feminine romantic vision, a view of life in which human passionate love is at the pivotal centre, an endorsement of Byron's 'Man's love is of man's life a thing apart, 'tis woman's whole existence'. Anthony Trollope (1815–1882) represents, on the other hand, an uncompromisingly masculine point of view, a preoccupation with and acceptance of the hierarchical nature of society, and an attitude towards the writing of fiction which is as completely practical as that of any tradesman or craftsman to the job in hand. He has been compared with, or been described as, a masculine version of Jane Austen: in that he lacked passion and poetry and was interested in nuances of social rank and behaviour there is some similarity but she was a far more subtle observer and she commanded a style of greater fastidiousness and economy. I find him, on the whole, an uninspiring writer, but must acknowledge the accumulative effectiveness of the Barset novels and the penetrating insights into the corruptive power of wealth in *The Way We Live Now*. For the triumphant fusion of what might loosely be called the masculine and feminine genius in the English novel, a fusion of the intuitive, passionate sensibility with vigour, intellectual curiosity, deep moral concern and a sense of form we must turn to the writings of George Eliot.

George Eliot

George Eliot (1819–1880) was born Mary Ann Evans and, from early youth, she showed formidable intellectual powers. Her early literary work was that of the translation of historical and philosophical works and the higher journalism, and in 1854 she formed a liason with a gifted man of letters and editor, George Henry Lewes, with whom she lived until his death in 1878 and from this fact alone – when we remember the restrictive moral climate of the period – it is clear that she was an unusually independent woman. From being a convinced and devout Christian she moved, in young womanhood, to a position of agnosticism and a firm belief in the importance of reason and moral choice. She was convinced that evil was not a metaphysical force but the consequence of acting perversely in opposition to the dictates

George Eliot   of rationally formulated principles of right and wrong. Genetic
and environmental factors might limit but could not eliminate
the possibility of choice.

Walter Allen, in his generally excellent book, *The
English Novel,* remarks that 'George Eliot's prose has neither
grace nor wit' and while I should concede that the rhythms of
her prose lack the fine surge and flow of Dickens, the ease
of Thackeray and the delicate chime of Jane Austen, her
sentences are packed with maximum thought and feeling, and
as for wit – far from being absent from her writing – it is one of
its distinguishing features. Of all her novels *Middlemarch*
(1871–72) and *Silas Marner* (1861) are, in their different ways,
the most satisfying and enjoyable and, for the reader who is
unfamiliar with George Eliot's work, I would recommend the
latter as an introduction, if only because it is a short book
compared with the very substantial *Middlemarch.*

Silas Marner is a linen-weaver who has come to the
village of Raveloe after he has been wrongly accused of theft
by the members of a non-conformist religious community of
which he has been a highly regarded member. The circumstances of his downfall have been such as to undermine his
Christian faith and in his solitary and industrious new life,
where he is avoided by most of the local inhabitants, for he
suffers from cataleptic fits which arouse superstitious fear and
suspicion, he begins to accumulate a hoard of gold which he
comes to worship with displaced religious fervour. The scene
in which he discovers that he has been robbed of his treasure
is a superb piece of imaginative writing, much of its power
being generated by a mixture of psychological perception and
empathetic identification with Marner's state of mind:

> He rose and placed his candle unsuspectingly on
> the floor near his loom, swept away the sand without
> noticing any change, and removed the bricks. The
> sight of the empty hole made his heart leap violently,
> but the belief that his gold was gone could not come at
> once – only terror, and the eager effort to put an end to
> the terror. He passed his trembling hand all about the
> hole, trying to think it possible that his eyes had
> deceived him; then he held the candle in the hole and
> examined it curiously, trembling more and more. At

last he shook so violently that he let fall the candle, and lifted his hands to his head, trying to steady himself, that he might think. Had he put his gold somewhere else, by a sudden resolution last night, and then forgotten it? A man falling into dark waters seeks a momentary footing even on sliding stones; and Silas, by acting as if he believed in false hopes, warded off the moment of despair. He searched in every corner, he turned his bed over, and shook it, and kneaded it; he looked in his brick oven where he laid his sticks. When there was no other place to be searched, he kneeled down again and felt once more all round the hole. There was no untried refuge left for a moment's shelter from the terrible truth.

Yes, there was a sort of refuge which always comes with the prostration of thought under an overpowering passion: it was that expectation of impossibilities, that belief in contradictory images, which is still distinct from madness, because it is capable of being dissipated by the external fact. Silas got up from his knees trembling, and looked round at the table: didn't the gold lie there after all? The table was bare. Then he turned and looked behind him – looked all round his dwelling, seeming to strain his brown eyes after some possible appearance of the bags where he had already sought them in vain. He could see every object in his cottage – and his gold was not there.

Again he put his trembling hands to his head, and gave a wild ringing scream, the cry of desolation. For a few moments after, he stood motionless; but the cry had relieved him from the first maddening pressure of the truth. He turned, and tottered towards his loom, and got into the seat where he worked, instinctively seeking this as the strongest assurance of reality.

Later in the novel Silas is more than compensated for the loss of his gold by the advent into his life of a little girl who finds her way to his cottage after her drunken mother has collapsed in a stupor to die of exposure in the snow. The development of the relationship between the child and the ageing miser is worked out with tenderness and considerable humour and George Eliot contrives, through the exercise of intelligence, wit and tact, to avoid the most common snare in Victorian literature, that of gross sentimentality.

George Eliot   *Middlemarch* is a massive and complex work with two major plots — the unhappy first marriage and subsequent successful one of Dorothea, and the crippled union of Lydgate, an idealistic young doctor, and the attractive but shallow and materialistic Rosamond Vincy — and two subordinate plots — the story of Mary Garth and the rise and fall of the hypocritical and dishonest banker, Bulstrode. Despite the vast breadth of the canvas the structure of the book is always under control and George Eliot's re-creation of Midlands provincial society at the time immediately preceding the first Reform Act of 1832 is solidly and richly comprehensive. Every character is observed with acute insight and even the lesser figures possess that capacity to surprise and convince which we associate with Dickens.

George Meredith

George Meredith   George Meredith (1828–1909) was, by the turn of the century, one of the most highly regarded novelists in the English language, but his reputation soon faded and as long ago as 1926 E. M. Forster in his Clark Lectures sponsored by Trinity College, Cambridge and published as *Aspects of the Novel* (1927), has this to say about him:

> Meredith is not the great name he was twenty or thirty years ago, when much of the universe and all Cambridge trembled . . . his visions of Nature – they do not endure like Hardy's, there is too much Surrey about them, they are fluffy and lush. He could no more write the opening chapter of *The Return of the Native* than Box Hill could visit Salisbury Plain. What is really tragic and enduring in the scenery of England was hidden from him, and so is what is really tragic in life. When he gets serious and noble-minded there is a strident overtone, a bullying that becomes distressing. I feel indeed that he was like Tennyson in one respect: through not taking himself quietly enough he strained his inside. And his novels: most of the social values are faked. The tailors are not tailors, the cricket matches are not cricket, the railway trains do not even seem to

be trains, the county families give the air of having
been only just that moment unpacked, scarcely in
position before the action starts, the straw still clinging
to their beards. It is surely very odd, the social scene in
which his characters are set; it is partly due to his
fantasy, which is legitimate, but partly a chilly fake,
and wrong. What with the faking, what with the
preaching, which was never agreeable and is now
said to be hollow, and what with the home counties
posing as the universe, it is no wonder Meredith now
lies in the trough.

It is true that Forster then goes on to praise Meredith's skill in
constructing plots, but any commendation after that 'home
counties posing as the universe' must be at least tinged with
the damnation of faint praise. Meredith is not always an easy
author to get into but his best work, of which *The Egoist* is
generally considered paramount, amply repays reading. The
plot, which Forster praises, is indeed cleverly constructed and
resolved but no novel can claim its readers' deep interest by
plot alone and Meredith's characterization, especially of the
women, is searching and his dialogue often sparkles.

The Egoist possesses many of the best qualities of
restoration comedy and the name of its central character,
Sir Willoughby Patterne, could comfortably appear in the
dramatis personae of any play by Congreve. Sir Willoughby is
rich and handsome but intolerably vain and selfish. The fact
that Laetitia Dale, who is clever and sensitive, should be in
love with him might exasperate the reader but it does not
strain credulity, for beautiful and intelligent women do fall for
conceited fools. Especially when the fools are rich and handsome, and Meredith has no difficulty in persuading us of this
unpalatable fact. Sir Willoughby is twice jilted by women
whom he regards as more suitable consorts before he finally
proposes to Laetitia who, to her credit, refuses him, though
subsequently changing her mind. Apart from the main
characters the portrayal of the lesser figures – which include
Dr Middleton, a professor who is based on Thomas Love
Peacock, Meredith's father-in-law – is executed with deft
economy.

Thomas Hardy

When in 1868 Meredith was established as a successful writer he read the manuscript of a first novel called *The Poor Man and the Lady* and he advised its author to abandon this work, which was too bitterly satirical, and write a story 'with a purely artistic purpose, giving it a more complicated plot'. The younger writer followed this advice, producing a novel that fairly bulged with plot and melodrama and it was duly published, though its author had to subsidize its publication. The novel was entitled *Desperate Remedies* (1871) and its author was Thomas Hardy (1840–1928).

Hardy's literary career spans the nineteenth and twentieth centuries but, as a novelist, he is a Victorian. His last novel, *Jude the Obscure,* was published in 1896. After its publication he devoted himself to writing the poetry which had always been his primary interest although his fiction had earned him reputation and considerable wealth. *Jude the Obscure* originally appeared as a monthly serial in *Harper's Magazine* between December, 1894 and November, 1895 and in this form he allowed editorial prudence to persuade him to make a number of cuts and modifications in the work as he had first written it. He excised references to Jude's being troubled by sexual desire and frustration, and the baby that is born to the unmarried hero and Sue Bridehead becomes, in the serial, an adopted child. When Arabella Donn fills Jude with strong drink he does not finish up in her bed but is decorously tucked up in a spare room. But when the novel came out Hardy had restored the original text and the book was condemned as a vicious attack on the sanctity of marriage, and the Bishop of Wakefield publicly proclaimed that he 'was so disgusted with its insolence and indecency that I threw it into the fire'. On hearing this Hardy commented that the holy man had burned the book only because he was no longer allowed to burn the author.

To readers of today it seems unbelievable that this novel could have seemed indecent (one wit referred to it as 'Jude the Obscene'). The seed of the book can be traced back to an entry in Hardy's diary for 1888 where a note appears referring to an idea for a short story about a young man who cannot afford to go to Oxford, '. . .his struggles and ultimate failure. Suicide. There is something this world ought to be shown, and I am the one to show it'. Obviously, this idea for a story developed into a full-length novel, and the original intention of showing the harsh frustrations endured by those whose intellectual and spiritual aspirations were cruelly obstructed by poverty and snobbishness was extended to embrace the further conflict between the desires of the spirit and the importunities of the flesh.

Jude the Obscure is a disturbing and, in parts, magnificently written novel but it is by no means flawless. The scene, towards the end of the book, where the elder of Jude's children hangs his little brother and sister and then himself, leaving the message, 'Done beacause we are too menny,' is excessively violent and sentimental in the manner of the weaker Victorian melodramas. The unrelieved darkness and bitterness of the whole work becomes finally too oppressive, so that the reader wants to protest that aesthetic and moral justice is not being done.

For my own taste Hardy's genius as a novelist find its fullest and most satisfying expression in *The Return of the Native* (1878) and *The Mayor of Casterbridge* (1886), where his poetic gifts for creating his own fictional world in the landscape of 'Wessex' are allied to an unflinching honesty of statement about human relationships and the fundamentally ironical nature of existence. Egdon Heath, in *The Return of the Native*, is, like Emily Brontë's moors in *Wuthering Heights*, a pervasive presence, both reality and symbol of the unchanging, indifferent, beautiful but heartless natural world. When Clym Yeobright, who is a diamond merchant in Paris, returns to his native Egdon, sick of the hollowness of his life in France, with the intention of becoming a schoolmaster, he marries Eustacia Vye who misguidedly hopes that he will take her to Paris. Yeobright's eyesight fails and to his wife's disgust he becomes a common labourer, a furze-cutter on the Heath, and Eustacia, in her disappointment, returns to her worthless lover, Wildeve. Here is a short extract from the scene in which Yeobright begins his humble work:

> His daily life was of a curious microscopic sort, his
> whole world being limited to a circuit of a few feet

Thomas Hardy

from his person. His familiars were creeping and winged things, and they seemed to enroll him in their band. Bees hummed around his ears with an intimate air, and tugged at the heath and furze-flowers at his side in such numbers as to weigh them down to the sod. The strange amber-coloured butterflies which Egdon produced, and which were never seen elsewhere, quivered in the breath of his lips, alighted upon his bowed back, and sported with the glittering point of his hook as he flourished it up and down. Tribes of emerald-green grasshoppers leaped over his feet, falling awkwardly on their backs, heads, or hips, like unskilful acrobats, as chance might rule; or engaged themselves in noisy flirtations under the fernfronds with silent ones of homely hue. Huge flies, ignorant of larders and wire-netting, and quite in a savage state, buzzed about him without knowing that he was a man. In and out of the fern-dells snakes glided in their most brilliant blue and yellow guise, it being the season immediately following the shedding of their old skins, when their colours are brightest. Litters of young rabbits came out from their forms to sun themselves upon hillocks, the hot beams blazing through the delicate tissue of each thin-fleshed ear, and firing it to a blood-red transparency in which the veins could be seen. None of them feared him.

Here we find Hardy's typical precision of descriptive detail which presents both the particulars of the external reality and his character's specific and revelatory response to it.

In the novels of Hardy a great deal of what had formerly been the exclusive territory of the poet has been invaded, the conscious control of his verbal rhythms, the creation and deployment of images and symbols. He is not the first novelist to introduce this poetic element: as we have seen it has been a feature in different ways of the methods of Emily Brontë, Dickens and of George Eliot. But in Hardy it becomes central to the effectiveness of the whole work and it is employed not only in his evocations of landscape, the weather and seasons, but in his creations of character. His description of Eustacia Vye presents an accurate representation of the physical presence of the woman but it works, too, mythopoeti-

cally, organically relating her to the inanimate world that she   **Thomas Hardy**
inhabits:

> She was in person full-limbed and somewhat heavy;
> without ruddiness, as without pallor; and soft to the
> touch as a cloud. To see her hair was to fancy that a
> whole winter did not contain darkness enough to form
> its shadow: it closed over her forehead like nightfall
> extinguishing the western glow.

In the next century, our own, we shall see how the achievements of Hardy and the great Victorians have been absorbed,
modified and elaborated by authors living in a more rapidly
changing society and being confronted by experiences different in degree and even in kind from anything that the earlier
writers had known. But before going on to the examination of
the novel during our own times we must take a brief look at
the earlier history of the novel in the United States, for the
interaction between the fiction of Britain and America cannot
be ignored by anyone interested in the novel of today.

5

THE EARLY AMERICAN NOVEL 1800–1900

The American novel as a distinctively indigenous product did not make its appearance until the nineteenth century was well under way. This is not to say that there were no novels published in the New World until James Fenimore Cooper (1789–1851) produced his tale of the American Revolution, *The Spy*, in 1821 and followed it with *The Pioneers* (1823) and the 'Leatherstocking Tales', the first of which, *The Last of the Mohicans* (1826), is the most famous today. During the last two decades of the eighteenth century a number of rather uninventive imitations of Richardson were written by authors who are now read, if at all, only for their historical interest, though Charles Brockden Brown succeeded in the task of importing from Britain and adapting the form of the gothic romance which served, to some extent, as a model for Edgar Allan Poe.

Brown was born in 1771 in Philadelphia and acquired what seems to have been a well merited reputation for youthful intellectual brilliance. He died of tuberculosis at the age of thirty-nine and between 1798 and 1801 he published six novels. *Wieland*, his first and probably his best, was written

within a month, and in it he contrived to combine the
Richardson formula of the seducer in merciless and obsessive
pursuit of the irreproachable heroine with the melodramatic
furnishings of the gothic horror tale. The villainous 'hero',
Carwin, who boasts among his many other gifts the rather surprising one of ventriloquism, is unprepossessing but fascinating with '. . .eyes lustressly black, and possessing, in the midst
of haggardness, a radiance inexpressibly serene and potent'.
He shows, too, that ambiguity of moral conduct, a conflict and
fusion of good and evil impulses, which is often a feature of
the romantic gothic hero so that, in the end, when he has
driven Wieland, the brother of the woman he is pursuing, to
madness he is able to prevent the lunatic from killing her.

James Fenimore Cooper

Far fewer British people, I imagine, have heard of – far less
read – Charles Brockden Brown than are familiar with the
name of Fenimore Cooper and it was the latter's distinction,
though not necessarily his intention, to have created a mythology which is essentially and exclusively American, for
the Leatherstocking Tales unquestionably prefigured the
innumerable elaborations, in both prose fiction and movies, of
the Western, or Cowboy and Indian adventure yarn. Natty
Bumpoo, the central character of these stories, is a 'white
woodsman' who represents to Cooper the finest kind of white
man, honourable, courageous and resourceful. He hates cities
and the corrupt values of material civilization and he finds, in
the American wilderness of the mid-eighteenth century, a
landscape and a way of life which is almost pre-lapsarian in its
innocence: he finds, too, in the person of Chingachgook, his
dark-skinned alter-ego, the noble savage to whom he is
joined by a bond of almost wordless but profound sympathy.

James
Fenimore
Cooper

    I suspect that Cooper is not much read today and his
Red Indian novels have acquired a reputation mainly as boys'
adventure stories. D. H. Lawrence, in his *Studies in Classic
American Literature*, has treated Cooper with great respect,
but Lawrence is more interested in the ideas which he extracts
from the tales than in the quality of the writing. In fact

James
Fenimore
Cooper

Cooper's style is awkward and verbose and his characterization clumsy. His importance lies in the fact that in his
fiction we find adumbrated themes which re-appear more
interestingly in later American novels, the division between
the dark primitive and instinctive aspects of human
consciousness and the rational, progressive intelligence, the
corruption of innocence by acquisitive experience.

Nathaniel Hawthorne

Nathaniel
Hawthorne

Nathaniel Hawthorne (1804–1864) was, in the opinion of
Henry James, America's first considerable literary artist, and
his best novels, *The Scarlet Letter* (1850) and *The House of the
Seven Gables* (1851) are both highly readable works of fiction
as well as important landmarks in the development of the
American novel. Hawthorne was deeply concerned with the
nature of evil and he could not accept the optimistic views of
the transcendentalist, Emerson, who believed that 'The World
is the mind precipitated.' In theory Hawthorne was opposed to
Puritan moral attitudes and believed in the redemptive power
of love – and, paradoxically, of hatred – for he saw with a
psychological astuteness remarkable in his time and place
that love can contain destructive impulses while hatred,
which may harbour disguised love, can produce beneficial
consequences. Yet despite his theoretical rejection of Puritanism, *The Scarlet Letter* is pervaded by an almost superstitious
fear of the powers of sexual passion.

The story is set in Boston, the Puritan New England of
the seventeenth century. An Englishman of advanced years
has sent his young wife there intending to follow her, but he is
captured by Indians and it is two years before he arrives to
find that Hester, his wife, is in the pillory with a baby in her
arms. She has refused to divulge the name of the father of the
child and after her punishment in the pillory she is sentenced
to wear, for the rest of her life, the letter 'A' signifying
'Adultress' embroidered on her bosom. Her husband, not
wishing to be associated with her and to be known as a
cuckold, assumes a new name, that of Roger Chillingworth,
and he extracts from Hester a promise that she will never

reveal his true identity. Hester and her baby daughter, Pearl, are at first ostracized and vilified by the community but gradually, through her good works, she wins respect while Chillingworth, who has set up practice as a physician, devotes himself to an obsessive quest to find out the identity of her lover. Pearl's father is in fact the Reverend Arthur Dimmesdale, the highly respected young minister whose moral cowardice has prevented him from admitting his guilt and sharing Hester's punishment. When Chillingworth does find this out he subjects Dimmesdale to long and subtle forms of mental torture from which the possibility of escape is presented when Hester, who still loves the minister, suggests that they flee to Europe. Dimmesdale finally rejects this temptation and publicly confesses his guilt on the pillory where Hester had been shamed and he dies in her arms.

The melodrama of the conclusion is made plausible by Hawthorne's artistry, by his evocation of the puritan ethos of seventeenth-century Boston, the harshness of its judgements and the sense of evil, hypocrisy and muffled sexuality which pervades the narrative. It is a short novel, a work of remarkable compression and power, and in the character of Hester the author portrays a woman of admirable courage, dignity and intelligence. Hester's strong sexual appeal, which is curiously inseparable from those virtues not usually associated with sexuality, is conveyed by means so subtle that they defy rational analysis. *The House of the Seven Gables*, which Hawthorne described as a book 'more proper and natural for me to write', is a well-constructed and stylish novel with a more optimistic and consolatory conclusion than *The Scarlet Letter* but it lacks the haunting power of the latter.

Herman Melville

Hawthorne was a contemporary and for a time, a friend and confidant of Herman Melville (1819–1891) who was born in New York City but, in 1830, moved to Albany where he worked as a clerk before going to sea at the age of eighteen. Back ashore in 1837 Melville became a schoolteacher but four years later he gave up this occupation and returned to sea,

**Herman
Melville**

shipping on the *Acushnet,* a whaling vessel bound for the South Pacific. This proved to be decisive for his future as a writer. In 1842 he deserted from the *Acushnet* at Nukuhiva in the Marquesas Islands and spent a few weeks among the cannibals in the Taipi Valley, from which experience he found the material for his first book, *Typee* (1846). He escaped from the Marquesas by joining the crew of an Australian whaler which took him to Tahiti where a similar vessel, *The Leviathan,* carried him to the Hawaiian Islands. There he enlisted on the frigate, *United States,* and found his way, via South America, to Boston where he was discharged in October 1844.

Typee and his second novel *Omoo* (1847) were both great successes in New York and London, and Melville, the gifted young sailor-author, was lionized by fashionable New York society. His third novel, *Mardi* (1849), attempted to be something more than a simple tale of adventure and its symbolist and literary ambitions did not meet with a sympathetic reception so Melville returned to more direct narratives with *Redburn* (1849) and *White-Jacket* (1850), both of which helped to restore his popularity. But financial reward and public reputation were not his only goals: Melville was an artist, a man haunted by a unique vision of reality and filled with the passion to give the vision shape and permanence in the form of the novel.

In 1850 Melville, now with a wife and son, moved to a Massachusetts farm where he was a neighbour of Hawthorne and it was there that he wrote his masterpiece, *Moby Dick* (1851), which was dedicated to the author of *The Scarlet Letter.* It was not a popular success and the insensitivity and incomprehension of its critics must have been heart-breaking to the author who had poured everything – passion, vision, knowledge, experience and skill – into this magnificient work. The rest of his life was increasingly unhappy. His strange and fascinating novel *Pierre* (1852), which explored the theme of incest, was no more popular than *Moby Dick* and though he continued to write in both verse and prose his reputation steadily declined until his death on September 28th, 1891.

Moby Dick is a work of complete originality, a tale of the sea crammed with factual information about whales and whaling, an allegory of good and evil, of man's quest for ultimate truth, a symbolic and poetic drama of infinite richness, a narrative in which humour and exciting action, philosophical speculation and pure poetry are intermingled. It tells the story of a single voyage on the whaler, the *Pequod,* whose captain, Ahab, is obsessed by his determination to destroy the white whale, Moby Dick, which has already, in a previous encounter, torn off his leg. The writing is heavily influenced by Shakespeare and the King James Bible but Melville succeeds in forging a style which is inimitably his own. It is a style which may, on first acquaintance, seem forbidding to a modern reader, but with a little perserverance the ear will attune itself to the swelling rhythms and harmonies which carry the narrative forwards as the great waves carry the *Pequod* to its violent destiny.

Moby Dick, like all great works of art, is universal in its imaginative depth and breadth but it is also specifically American in its attitude to human existence, its response to life and the problems of good and evil. This attitude is at once Calvinistic yet in rebellion against its own allegiance to those inflexible moral laws. Melville is irresistibly drawn to the dark opposites of orthodox moral desiderata. It is a book of such extraordinary originality that it is difficult to see precisely how it has influenced succeeding American novelists, though there can be few of any stature who have not at some time fallen beneath its spell.

**Herman
Melville**

Mark Twain

The case of Melville's younger contemporary, Mark Twain (1835–1910), is quite different, for his outstanding work, *Huckleberry Finn,* published in 1885, has been part of American mythology and its influence may be clearly discerned in authors as different from each other as Ernest Hemingway and J. D. Salinger.

Mark Twain

Mark Twain was born Samuel Langhorne Clemens in Florida, Missouri, the son of a disreputable Virginian who died when the boy was twelve. Young Samuel was apprenticed as a printer to his brother, Orion, a newspaper publisher,

Mark Twain and later he travelled from the Middle West to New York, sending back letters to his brother, who published them in his newspaper. He then set out on a journey to South America but ended up on the Mississippi as a river pilot, this occupation coming to an end after four years when, at the outbreak of the Civil War, he enlisted in the Confederate Army. His company was disbanded after only a few weeks and instead of re-enlisting he joined Orion in Nevada. He began contributing to the *Territorial Enterprise* and adopted the nom-de-plume of 'Mark Twain' which was derived from the leadsman's shout on the Mississippi riverboats when his craft was drawing two fathoms and was therefore in safe waters.

By the time he was in his early thirties Twain had achieved popularity as a lecturer, comic writer and journalist and with the publication of *Innocents Abroad* (1869) and his marriage to a beautiful heiress, Olivia Langdon, in 1870, he settled down in Hartford to his career as a professional author. In 1872 he published *Roughing It* which was based on his Nevada experiences and in 1873 *The Gilded Age*, a satire on corruption in business and political life of the period following the Civil War. Between 1876 and 1883 he produced *Tom Sawyer, A Tramp Abroad, The Prince and the Pauper* and *Life on the Mississippi* and then, in 1885, his masterpiece, *Huckleberry Finn*.

It is an interesting fact that two of the most widely known nineteenth-century American novels – *The Last of the Mohicans* and *Huckleberry Finn* – are popularly known as boys' adventure stories, but before we begin to make careless assumptions from this about the adolescent nature of American culture we in Britain should recall that *Robinson Crusoe* and *Gulliver's Travels* are also widely thought of as books for children. Nevertheless there is in *Huckleberry Finn* a quality of innocence which is absent from most European fiction and we find in its pages a paradigm of the American Dream of a world in which the possibility of perfect human equality and happiness is an attainable reality. It is the first American novel which is written in the vernacular and Twain's use of the vocabulary and rhythms of common speech is an artistic triumph. Ernest Hemingway has said, 'All modern American literature comes out of one book by Mark

Twain called *Huckleberry Finn* and, if this statement is too **Mark Twain**
sweeping, it still contains a good deal of truth. However, there
are, very broadly speaking, two kinds of American novel: one
which, like *Huckleberry Finn*, has its imaginative roots firmly
planted in the American soil and which is written in the
language of its people, and the other which looks towards
Europe for its models and is more concerned with the
aesthetic problems of formal elegance and style. Henry James
(1843–1916), one of the finest novelists in the English
language, was of the second kind.

Henry James

Henry James was born in New York City of wealthy and **Henry James**
cultured parents and was educated, at first privately, then at
various schools until 1855 when the family spent three years
in Europe, returning to live at Newport, Rhode Island, for a
year before going back for another shorter stay in Europe. In
1862 he entered the Harvard Law School but he soon
abandoned his legal studies to devote himself to writing. After
1866 he lived mainly in Paris, Rome and London and for the
last twenty years of his life – towards the end of which (in
1915) he became a naturalized British subject – he lived at
Lamb House, Rye, in Sussex.

The main influences on his early work were Balzac,
Dickens and Hawthorne, about whom he wrote a perceptive
study, but during his residence in Paris in the seventies he met
and became interested in the work of Flaubert and Turgenev
and his concern with style and structure in the novel became
almost obsessive. The principal preoccupation of his seventies
novels, which include *Roderick Hudson* (1876), *The American*
(1877), *Daisy Miller* (1879) and *Portrait of a Lady* (1881), is the
interrelationship of America and Europe with the first
symbolizing Innocence and the second, Experience. After the
publication of *Portrait of a Lady*, arguably his finest novel, the
chief concern of his fiction was with the complexities of the
artist's relation to life which he explored in *The Tragic Muse*
(1890) and *The Spoils of Poynton* (1897), and his later novels
continued to refine the art of fiction to a point where, in the

Henry James   opinion of some critics, the work becomes too far removed from the common ground of quotidian human experience, exquisitely wrought but lacking the tang, vigour and variety of the streets and marketplace.

paleface and redskin

**paleface
and
redskin**   Mark Twain, the robust humorous writer of tales in the vernacular of the American West, a realist whose allegories or myths of good and evil flowered from his imaginative recapturing and exploration of his own early life, and Henry James, cultured, sophisticated artist whose symbolic narratives consciously analysed in marmoreal prose the predicament of the American in Europe, rootlessness and innocence confronted by tradition and experience, are the two main sources from which subsequent American fiction has proceeded. An American critic, Philip Rahv, in an essay entitled 'Paleface and Redskin' published in the 1940s, divided his country's authors into two opposing types: the redskin whose work dealt with the primitive life of the frontier or the concrete wilderness of the big city, and the paleface who wrote of the cultural middle-class environment of the East. The redskin, descendant of Twain, used vigorous demotic language showing no respect, if not open contempt, for high cultural values and gloried in his Americanism, his tough independence and realism. The paleface, for whom the major art of Europe stood as both exemplar and reproach, acknowledged James, the conscious formalist, as master and valued the traditional virtues of the Old World, intellectual control and elegance of style and structure. While this kind of classification is crudely oversimplified we can recognize how it came to be formulated though, as we shall see, the redskin and paleface were often to intermarry and to produce, in the twentieth century, novels that are distinctively American. In fact, before the nineteenth century had ended, three novelists had achieved something approaching a synthesis of the two traditions in their striving to produce fiction which reflected the social changes operating in their country, the growth of the large cities and the effects of the transition from a rural to an urban existence.

It reflected, too, changes in the intellectual climate, the weakening of prescribed moral and religious certainties and the spreading influence of a more pragmatic, determinist view of human conduct.

the naturalists

The three authors – Hamlin Garland (1860–1940), Frank Norris (1870–1902) and Stephen Crane (1871–1900) – had all been influenced by the work of Émile Zola (1840–1902), the French novelist and leader of the 'naturalist' school in his own country who believed passionately in scientific determinism, that environment and heredity were decisive forces in the shaping of personality and individual destiny, and that it was the novelist's task to demonstrate these forces in operation through a detached and completely truthful representation of the objective world. Hamlin Garland was born on a Wisconsin farm but he escaped from the drudgery of agricultural work and became a teacher and writer in Boston. In 1893 he moved from Boston to Chicago, finding in this city an exciting manifestation of the transition between the old world and the new. *A Little Norsk* (1892) is a harshly realistic account of the life of a Dakota farm girl and in *The Rose of Dutcher's Coolly* (1895) he rather more interestingly shows the intellectual and imaginative development of Rose Dutcher who is brought up by her widowed father on a Wisconsin farm but, after her graduation at the State University, leaves her home for Chicago where she hopes to achieve success as a writer. She is courted by the wealthy Elbert Harvey but is attracted to Warren Mason, a literary critic and editor, though both are at first afraid that marriage would mean the loss of the freedom that each so deeply values. Garland is readable, though even his best work is marred by cliché of style and situation: the descriptions of the poor farmsteads are vividly drawn and the reductive power of poverty and monotonous labour is conveyed with sharp authenticity.

Frank Norris was born in Chicago but moved at the age of fourteen to San Francisco and a year later was sent to Paris to study art. On his return from Europe he attended the

University of California (1890–94) where he began to write short stories in verse but, influenced by his reading of Zola, he soon began a naturalist novel set in San Francisco, *McTeague* (1899). In 1898 he visited Cuba to report on the progress of the Spanish-American War for *McClure's Magazine* and on his return to the USA he embarked on a trilogy, the 'Epic of the Wheat'. The first volume of the trilogy, *The Octopus* was to deal with the cultivation of wheat in California and the struggle of the ranchers against the railroad; the second, *The Pit*, was to be a story of speculation in the Chicago Wheat Exchange and the third, *The Wolf* – the writing of which was prevented by his sudden death – was to be about a famine-stricken European village.

McTeague is a study in moral degeneration. McTeague is an unqualified dentist who meets Trina Sieppe through her cousin Marcus Schouler, is attracted by and marries her. Trina wins five thousand dollars in a lottery and Schouler, who had hoped to marry her himself, feels irrationally that he has been cheated, not so much of his bride as of her money. Vengefully he exposes McTeague as an unlicensed quack and the marriage declines into squalor and misery. McTeague murders his wife and flees, pursued by Schouler and in attempting to cross Death Valley he kills his pursuer though not before Schouler has managed to handcuff their wrists together. So McTeague is condemned to die of thirst, chained to the corpse of the man who is at least partly responsible for his downfall.

As Norris says of McTeague and Trina, 'Chance had brought them face to face, and mysterious instincts as ungovernable as the winds of heaven were at work knitting their lives together.' This authorial attitude might seem similar to the fatalism of Thomas Hardy, except that Norris does not subscribe to any supernatural view of fate: the destructive powers are inherent in the characters – sexual desire, greed and envy. In *The Octopus* we see the irresistible forces of greed in wider, economic terms, ruining not just individuals but society itself. The Pacific and Southwestern Railroad dominates the State government and makes conditions intolerable for the wheat-farmers whose rebellion is inevitably ineffectual. Just as individuals are at the mercy of the self-destructive impulses fostered by nature or environment, so communities are victimized by economic laws and circumstances.

Stephen Crane

Of the three naturalistic novelists Stephen Crane is perhaps the most interesting and congenial to modern readers, though of his surprisingly abundant output – he died of tuberculosis at the age of twenty-eight – only *The Red Badge of Courage* and his short story, *The Open Boat,* will probably be widely known today. He was born in New Jersey and attended Lafayette College and Syracuse University, spending one year at each before moving to New York City where he began his first book while scraping a living as a freelance journalist. His first novel, *Maggie, A Girl of the Streets*, was too uncompromisingly grim to find a publisher and when he borrowed money from his brother to issue it privately it met with no success. Then he produced his *The Red Badge of Courage* (1895), an astonishing imaginative feat, a realistic study of a young soldier's first experience of the battlefields of the Civil War written by a youthful author whose only knowledge of military action was derived from his reading of factual accounts of that campaign and of Tolstoy's novel, *War and Peace.* The book was a great success and its popularity led to the re-issue of *Maggie* and Crane's reputation was made.

The Red Badge of Courage deals with Henry Fleming (usually referred to in the book simply as 'the youth' or 'he') and his responses to the experiences of battle. At the beginning he shows the common attitudes of the raw recruit, an eagerness to taste action and prove himself a hero, a boastful affectation of indifference to impending danger. When he is immersed in the maelstrom of battle he is overwhelmed by fear and panic and he runs away and joins the wounded behind the lines. There he witnesses the hideous death of his wounded friend, Jim Conklin, and his shame of not bearing an honourable wound – the 'red badge' of the title – is increased. Later he shows great courage in combat and emerges from the ordeal both chastened and strengthened.

Stephen Crane

The Red Badge of Courage is a naturalistic account of the realities of war but it makes, too, an implicit comment on the nature of physical courage and cowardice and presents a determinist view of human behaviour. Henry Fleming's moment of heroism is an unconsidered reaction to events, almost a conditioned reflex, not essentially different from his running away. The circumstances of battle are presented – though this is not explicitly stated – as a microcosm of the larger conflict of life itself in which the individual behaves according to impulses and responses over which he has little control. Crane, in this novel, foreshadowed the work of Hemingway and Scott Fitzgerald, fiction which faithfully reflects the physical realities of the world inhabited by its characters but which also carries, beneath the naturalistic surfaces, deeper symbolic significance.

6

THE NOVEL IN BRITAIN 1900–1960

We have so far glanced briefly at the development of the novel in Britain and America from its beginnings to the end of the nineteenth century. Now that we have reached the twentieth century even greater selectivity will have to be exercised because of the sheer quantity of novels in the English language produced during the period. Obviously I shall have to choose those authors who stand conspicuously above their contemporaries either for the sheer brilliance and power of their individual books or for their historical importance as technical innovators who have succeeded in enlarging the scope of the novel itself. The choice of the first must be to some extent determined by my own tastes and preferences but I shall do my best to modify these by heeding the judgements of the orthodox critical opinion of our time. I shall not omit reference to a novelist who is recognized as a major figure because I personally find his or her writings uncongenial, nor shall I include authors simply because they have given me pleasure unless this enjoyment is accompanied by a conviction that their works possess durable literary quality and this conviction is endorsed by the authority of other novelists and the best critics.

Joseph Conrad

Joseph Conrad Paradoxically the first indisputably major English novelist of the present century was not an Englishman but a Pole who adopted our language and became a naturalized British subject. His anglicized name was Joseph Conrad (1857–1924) and he was born Teodor Josef Konrad Korzeniowski in the Ukraine, of Polish parents. The family moved to Vologda in Northern Russia and Josef attended school at Krakow until, in 1874, he became a sailor in the French Merchant Navy, thereby fulfilling an ambition which he had held from early boyhood. In 1878 he joined the crew of a British vessel after which he sailed only in British ships, mainly in the Far East, and in 1884, the year of his naturalization, he gained his Board of Trade Master's certificate. He continued to sail the seas until 1894 when he settled down ashore to a life of authorship.

Conrad had been taught French in his childhood and he had read widely in this language but he did not begin to learn English until he was twenty-three years of age. The fact that he mastered the tongue so thoroughly that he became one of the leading English novelists not only of his own generation but in the entire history of our literature is astounding and, of course, far more than extraordinary linguistic skill alone was necessary for this achievement. On the surface, his novels are adventure stories which, for the authenticity of their background, call upon his experiences at sea and in foreign lands, but they are also intricately constructed works of art and he uses the tale of action to explore and illuminate dark recesses of the human heart and mind. *Lord Jim* (1900), for example, tells the story of the young first mate of the battered old steamer which is carrying a crowd of pilgrims on their way to Mecca, and his moment of panic when the ship is in danger of sinking and he jumps into the sea to save himself from going down with the craft. The rest of the novel shows Jim's quest for self-redemption and, when he becomes the ruler of a remote district in Malaya, an office which he discharges with justice and probity, it seems that at last he can expiate his guilt for that one moment of weakness. But his little territory is invaded by an English criminal and his gang, and again Jim is exposed to moral pressures which he is not

fully equipped to face though he does in the end redeem him- **Joseph Conrad**
self through self-sacrifice.

Conrad's style is carefully wrought though at times it carries a certain clumsiness or unexpectedness of rhythm, and some of the speech-patterns do not quite fall into the shapes of idiomatic English conversation, but his descriptions, especially those of the darker moods of nature and the terror unleashed by tumultuous seas, are executed with great power. *Nostromo* (1904), which is generally accepted as his best novel, is a work of tremendous richness and complexity and it shows his structural, analytic and imaginative gifts at their best. In this novel he invents a country, the South American Republic of Costaguana with its great silver mine at San Tomé. The imagined country is convincingly created and it serves Conrad as a microcosm of the modern world of capitalist and imperialist exploitation and the corruptive power of wealth. Even Nostromo, the noble leader and man of honour, is corrupted and finally destroyed by the silver which dominates the lives of all the characters in the book.

The Secret Agent (1907) demonstrates Conrad's extraordinary thematic range and it is the fore-runner of the novels of espionage which later were to become so popular, but like the rest of his writings it is far more than a thriller, although it can be read with pleasure at that level alone. The scenes in the seedy backstreets of late Victorian London, the newspaper shop where the revolutionaries hold their meetings, the Home Secretary of the House of Commons and the high-ranking police official are realistically presented yet Conrad is using this setting to show how even the apparently stable structure of society at that time is constantly menaced by subversive and destructive forces, that our sense of security as individuals and members of the body politic is an illusion, that our great cities are no safer than the primitive jungles.

Conrad, as we have seen, was a conscious artist, a craftsman deeply concerned with the possibilities of the novel as aesthetic artefact and, despite his love of England and his adoption of British nationality, he remained an exotic, a polyglot, who was regarded with suspicion by his neighbours because of his 'foreign' manners, especially his habit of kissing the hand of a lady on being introduced. H. G. Wells

Joseph Conrad and Arnold Bennet were, in their different ways, as English as tea and muffins, though neither, it seems from their biographies, was averse to kissing – and a good deal more than merely kissing – ladies, if less ceremoniously and more secretively than it was Conrad's practice.

H. G. Wells

H. G. Wells H. G. Wells (1866–1946) was born at Bromley in Kent, the son of a professional cricketer. He proved to be a clever youth and while working, first as a draper's assistant and then as an assistant schoolmaster, he won a scholarship to the Royal College of Science, South Kensington, and graduated B.Sc., in 1888. He taught until 1893 after which he devoted himself to writing, publishing the *Time Machine* in 1895, the first of his science-fiction romances, the success of which was repeated with the *Invisible Man* (1897), *The War of the Worlds* (1898) and *The First Men in the Moon* (1901). But these stories, excellent though they were and still eminently readable today, do not show Wells at the height of his powers as a novelist. The books which are most likely to provide and which offer the greatest enjoyment to modern readers are the comic novels conceived firmly in the tradition of Fielding and Dickens, *Love and Mr Lewisham* (1900), *Kipps* (1905) and *The History of Mr Polly* (1910) and, of these, the last named is the most accomplished and pleasurable.

Mr Polly is an endearing character, the little man in revolt against the dullness, pettiness and squalor of contemporary life. His adventures are related with affection and gusto and the reader quickly comes to see Mr Polly as a true hero, a man who despite his social and physical disadvantages is possessed of a noble imagination and real moral and physical courage. The plot of the novel is inventive and the characterization, even of the minor figures, is solidly achieved. I do not think it would be too much to claim that in *The History of Mr Polly* we find a synthesis of the picaresque vitality of Fielding and the imaginative and psychological depth of Dickens, a synthesis which he was never quite able to repeat though, in *Tono-Bungay* (1909), there are splendid moments, particularly in the earlier pages where Wells describes the life of a boy in the servants' hall of a great Victorian home.

The boy, George Ponderevo, has an uncle, an obscure chemist who invents a useless patent medicine called Tono-Bungay and makes a vast fortune. The adventures of Uncle Ponderevo encompass Well's wide range of concerns: there are passages of broad comedy, elements of science-fiction and a satirical analysis of the capitalist system which not only permits but encourages the kind of fraud that the little chemist so successfully perpetrates. The novel weakens its grip towards the end when both content and style become perfunctory, almost as if the author has tired of the characters and situations he has created. In a letter written in 1915 to Henry James he stated, 'I had rather be called a journalist than an artist' and, while allowing for the exaggeration of ill-temper (he was quarrelling with James at the time), there is no doubt that his ambitions as historical prophet and surgeon of Western civilization's diseases, his fascination with abstract political, scientific and philosophical ideas did result in a diminution of his powers as a purely imaginative author.

Arnold Bennett

Arnold Bennett (1867–1931) was much more of a committed literary artist than Wells though he was also a shrewd man of practical affairs who was quite prepared to write on occasion simply for financial reward. He was born near Hanley in Staffordshire and became a solicitor's clerk in London but soon established himself in journalism, at first becoming assistant editor and then editor of the magazine *Woman,* and later building a formidable reputation as a theatrical and literary critic. His standing as a novelist is based chiefly on *The Old Wives' Tale* (1908) and the 'Clayhanger' series consisting of three novels, *Clayhanger* (1910), *Hilda Lessways* (1911) and *These Twain* (1916) which in 1925 were published in a single volume entitled *The Clayhanger Family.* The background for these novels, presented with detailed and vivid accuracy, are the 'Five Towns' of Tunstall, Burslem, Hanley,

**Arnold
Bennett**

Stoke-upon-Trent and Longton, centres of the Midlands pottery industry and now incorporated in the borough of Stoke-on-Trent.

The Old Wives' Tale, generally regarded as Bennett's major achievement, is set in Paris and Burslem. It is a work in the tradition of naturalist fiction and it tells the story of two sisters, Constance and Sophia Baines, who are the daughters of a Midlands draper. Constance, who is a prudent and decorous young woman, marries Samuel Povey, the chief assistant in the draper's shop, and settles down to an uneventful life in Bursley (the fictional counterpart of Burslem) but Sophia, more headstrong and passionate, elopes with Gerald Scales, a commercial traveller who comes into a fortune, and they leave England for Paris. Scales is a vicious character and he deserts his wife who has to survive in the foreign capital as a lodging-house keeper. At the end of the book the two sisters, now old ladies, are re-united to see out the rest of their days in Bursley. Bennett portrays not only the principal characters but the changing features of their background with scrupulous fidelity: the realism, which embraces incidents of triviality, comedy and pathos, is illumined by a steady glow of sympathy and shows the author, at his best, to be one of the most gifted of his generation.

The realistic provincialism of Bennett's fiction, his ability to find excitement and even beauty in the ordinary, unglamorous, sometimes squalid environment of a Midlands industrial town, was to influence many later English novelists and its presence may clearly be seen in the popular regional novels of the fifties and sixties, notably in John Braine's over-rated *Room at the Top*, Alan Sillitoe's *Saturday Night and Sunday Morning* and Stan Barstow's *A Kind of Loving*. But the novel as a more or less serious art form was, in the early decades of the present century, mainly a product of authors of middle-class origins writing for a middle-class readership. Despite the Education Acts of 1870 and 1876 bare literacy was by no means ubiquitous among the working classes and it was not until H. A. L. Fisher's act of 1918 that compulsory schooling until the age of 14 was effectively established. John Galsworthy (1867–1933), the author of the still popular *Forsyte Saga*, Somerset Maugham (1874–1965), Saki (H. H.

Munro) (1870–1916) and Hugh Walpole (1884–1941) all came   **Arnold**
from affluent middle-class backgrounds and were educated at   **Bennett**
expensive public schools, though one of the finest novelists
of that period came in fact from an extraordinarily
unconventional and exotic family environment. This writer
was Ford Madox Ford (1873–1939) whose remarkable gifts
have not yet received the full critical homage that they merit.

Ford Madox Ford

Born Ford Madox Hueffer, Ford Madox Ford was the son of   **Ford**
Francis Hueffer, the music critic of *The Times,* and grandson   **Madox Ford**
of Ford Madox Brown, the painter who was associated with
the Pre-Raphaelites though not an official member of the
Brotherhood. Ford changed his name in 1919 for various
reasons, the strongest of which was his desire to start a new
life after the end of the First World War during which he had
served in the British Army but suffered some embarrassment
from his German patronymic. His excellence as a novelist has
perhaps been partly obscured by the wide variety of his other
activities and achievements. He was a brilliant, sympathetic
and generous editor and in 1908 he founded the *English
Review,* a monthly journal which published the work of
Hardy, Henry James, Galsworthy and H. G. Wells as well as
the first short stories of D. H. Lawrence. He wrote poetry,
literary and art criticism, history, biography, fairy stories for
children, political polemics and autobiography and his vast
output of fiction includes historical romances, satire, farce and
two novels written in collaboration with Joseph Conrad. It
could be said with some justification that he wrote too much
and it is doubtful whether many of the 70 or so works now
unavailable will ever be reprinted. Perhaps this will be no
great loss but at least one of his novels, *The Good Soldier*
(1915) could claim to be among the very few great novels of
this century; *The Fifth Queen* trilogy (1906–8) is superb
historical fiction and the first three Tietjens stories (a fourth,
less impressive one was added but can, I think, be ignored)
Some Do Not (1924), *No More Parades* (1925) and *A Man
Could Stand Up* (1926) are absorbing and delightful works.

**Ford
Madox Ford**

The Good Soldier is a study of the relationship between four people, two married couples, narrated by one of the husbands who is being continuously deceived by all three of the other actors in the drama. Ashburnham – 'the good soldier' of the title – is a man who possesses all the virtues of courage, generosity, honesty, apparent purity of mind, but these qualities are negated or contaminated by a single moral flaw: he is an incorrigible womanizer to whom the presence of any desirable and available female becomes an irresistible challenge. His wife, Leonora, seems devoted to him and she behaves in public as if their marriage is happy and secure but in private scarcely acknowledges his existence. Dowell, the narrator, is – at least on the surface – a naive American, an innocent and hopelessly bemused observer whose own wife Florence is, beneath her frivolous and childish manner, a monster of depravity and deceit. She is having an affair with Ashburnham and both of them are supposed to be suffering from a heart disease though in fact they are both malingering; their lying about their hearts in the literal, medical sense, is an index to the deeper lies each tells about the heart in the metaphorical, romantic sense, and one of the themes of this richly complex novel is the destructive power of falsehood, the overt calculated lying of Florence and the more insidious, emotional lying of Ashburnham, his chronic sentimentality.

The Good Soldier possesses all the complexity, contradictoriness, shadow, darkness and light of life itself; it is funny and desperately sad, vibrant with pity, passion and horror. The principal characters, as in the Tietjens books, are all from the middle class, their freedom from harassment by the problems and struggles presented by poverty allows them, and their author, to concentrate on their emotional, moral and spiritual lives in a way that would lack veracity in a different, harsher milieu.

E. M. Forster

E. M. Forster

E. M. Forster (1879–1970) wrote almost exclusively about the middle classes too, and unlike Ford his own early background was completely conventional. He was educated at Tonbridge School and King's College, Cambridge, though later he travelled a good deal, spending considerable periods in Italy, Egypt and India.

Forster's career as a novelist is a strange one. In his very long life he published only five novels, the last of which, *A Passage to India,* as long ago as 1924 *(Maurice,* a novel dealing with homosexuality, was brought out after his death) yet his reputation was never eclipsed, indeed, as one critic remarked, it seemed to increase with each book he did not write. The great popularity of his work is easy to understand. There is a feeling of human warmth in all of his writing, a ready sympathy for all forms of suffering and distress, a tolerance towards and understanding of characters whose personalities, motivations and aspirations would seem hostile to his own. He is a splendid story-teller and the plots of all of his novels are satisfyingly constructed, full of incident and suspense. His style is unfussy, direct and strongly individual and he has a highly developed sense of the comic and the ironic.

All five novels are eminently readable but there can be little doubt that *Howards End* (1910) and *A Passage to India* are the most accomplished. *Howards End* is an engrossing story, full of penetrating characterization, passages of humour, pathos and surprising twists of fortune and circumstance including an especially shocking death, and it contains what could reasonably be described as Forster's philosophical and moral position as a liberal humanist who believed that apparently opposing attitudes and beliefs among individuals and in society could be and should be reconciled and that such reconciliation would be fruitful and salutary. In the novel the liberal, sensitive and imaginative values are embodied in the Schlegel sisters, Margaret and Helen, and their brother, Tibby, who are devoted to living the civilized 'good life', cherishing the arts, music, literature and amateur philosophical speculation and conversation; the world of practical affairs, materialistic common-sense, suspicion of emotion and imagination is represented by the Wilcoxes, father and son, and a marriage takes place between Margaret Schlegel and the elder Wilcox, a union which is viewed with dismay by the other members of both families.

Enjoyable as it is *Howards End* is not entirely successful, either as a symbolic representation of English society and

E. M. Forster   its divisions or as a realistic study in conflicting attitudes and
characters. Neither the Schlegels nor the Wilcoxes are strong
or complex enough to carry the symbolic weight they are
called upon to bear and Forster's introduction of characters
from the working class – or, more accurately, from the very
lowest rung of the lower middle-class – in the persons of the
clerk Leonard Bast, and his awful mistress Jacky, shows some
failure in observation. In certain respects Leonard is brilliantly
drawn: he is a type who is instantly recognizable, humourless,
solemnly ambitious, not so much for material success as
intellectual and social status. He reads Ruskin and attends
symphony concerts not because he derives pleasure from
these activities but because he believes they will 'improve'
him. Where Forster fails to convince us of Leonard's reality is
in the passages of direct speech in which it becomes quite
obvious that the author has either never heard the talk of such
people or, if he has, he fails dismally to capture its rhythms,
idioms and syntax.

A *Passage to India* suffers from no such weakness,
partly because all of the characters are based upon types with
whom Forster was very familiar but more importantly he was
able to focus far more sharply on his main theme, the irreconcilable differences between East and West. The central
incident of the plot is the expedition to the Caves of Marabar
organized for a group of British visitors by the young Muslim
doctor, Aziz, who is a passionate admirer of the British.
Among the visitors is Adela Quested, young, earnest and
rather unattractive, who is determined to explore and understand the 'real India' and overcome the impediments and
taboos erected by the snobbishness and intolerance of her
countrymen. This young woman hysterically accuses Aziz of
assaulting her in the caves and he is arrested and brought to
trial. The resolution of this drama is ambiguous: Adela suddenly and without explanation withdraws the charge and Aziz
is freed but, not unnaturally, he is embittered against the
British. The other characters are all excellently delineated,
especially the powerful and equivocal figure of Mrs Moore
who, though apparently an ordinary enough old lady, seems
to possess remarkably intuitive insights into the sources of
conflict in India.

the 'experimental' novel

Both Forster and Ford Madox Ford were, of course, skilled craftsmen, each in his different way deeply concerned with the potentialities of the novel as an artistic form, but neither was 'experimental' in any radical way. In the hands of these two gifted writers the English novel continued to develop: it became an instrument of great subtlety and suppleness, but its line of descent from the eighteenth century of Richardson and Fielding through the more sophisticated developments of Jane Austen, Dickens, George Eliot, Meredith and Henry James may easily be traced. But in the period immediately following the First World War the intellectual and spiritual climate in Britain, as elsewhere, had undergone a profound change. The psychological theories of Freud and his associates were becoming widely influential; technological advances were altering the tempo of existence, radio and film were becoming important means of communication and, following the Impressionists, came the Cubists, the Futurists and the Surrealists, all of whom were in revolt against the artistic orthodoxies of the day and resolved to extend the limits of their medium. It was inevitable that literature, too, should be affected by the Zeitgeist and in the 1920s the works of two crucially experimental and influential novelists were published, novels which, though rooted firmly in the traditional English or European Novel, were startlingly original in the ways in which they extended the art of narrative. These novelists were Virginia Woolf and James Joyce.

Virginia Woolf

Virginia Woolf (1882–1941) believed that the traditional English naturalistic novel, especially in its later manifestations in the works of Wells and Bennett, though it dealt in painstaking detail with the surfaces or the appearances of things and people, failed to capture the true reality, the quiddity of things – of human character and personality. For her the

Virginia
Woolf

conventions of chronological narrative, plot and description, the need for a beginning, middle and end to the story, to provide comedy or tragedy or love interest, were impediments to the possibility of re-creating life itself. 'Is life like this?' she asked in an essay in *The Common Reader*. 'Must novels be like this?' And she answered these questions with a resounding negative and set out in her own fiction to dispense with most of the traditional means of the novelist and explore pure states of consciousness. She eliminated from her work the authorial or narrative voice and wrote, as it were, from within the mind and sensibility of her characters, aiming at capturing that seemingly irrational, capricious flow of disconnected impressions, images and ideas that together form our inner and – Virginia Woolf would say – our true experience of life. This method of writing came to be known as 'stream of consciousness', a term that was probably first used by a reviewer, the novelist May Sinclair, who was discussing not Virginia Woolf, but a writer who anticipated, though less resourcefully, Woolf's artistic aims, Dorothy Richardson (1873–1957).

The debate as to the stature of Virginia Woolf still goes on today. Her best novels are *Mrs Dalloway* (1922), *To The Lighthouse* (1927), and *The Waves* (1931) and each of these contains exquisite passages of reflection and perception. But my own feeling is that she was debarred from truly major achievement by the extreme narrowness, not only of her aesthetic purposes, but of the range of experience and characters with which she deals. Her intention is to record the most intense moments of response to the ordinary stimuli of quotidian life but the characters who respond are always middle-class intellectuals of the most refined sensibility, people in fact very like herself. There is an almost total absence of the animal vigour, the struggle, sweat, passion and comedy of life as most of us know it. Virginia Woolf creates her own world but it is a world of distilled emotions, fugitive radiances, intangible threats. It is not the world of the market-place, work, pubs, domestic joy and tribulation and dramatic conflict and reconciliation, and here she is quite unlike the other great experimental novelist, James Joyce.

James Joyce and *Ulysses*

James Augustine Aloysius Joyce (1882–1941) was born in
Dublin and educated at Jesuit schools and at University
College, Dublin. He became disillusioned with what he
regarded as the bigotry of Irish Catholicism and the stifling
atmosphere of provincial bohemian life in the capital and in
1902 he spent a year in Paris. He returned only briefly to
Ireland after which he left to spend the rest of his life in exile,
mainly in Trieste, Zurich and Paris, where he made a frugal
living by teaching English, suffering prolonged and
harrowing poverty as well as severe distress from eye-trouble.
His great novel, *Ulysses*, was first published in Paris in 1922
but it was not available in England until 1937, four years after
it had been cleared of charges of obscenity in the United
States District Court.

    Ulysses is almost certainly the most complex single
work of imaginative literature ever to be written and since its
publication innumerable books and theses have been produced by critics and scholars all over the world who have set
out to analyse and elucidate the layers of meaning and inter-
pret the symbols and allegories it contains. There is no doubt
that it is a very difficult book but readers should not be over-
intimidated for it yields immense delight even when imper-
fectly understood. The novel deals with the events occurring
during a single day in Dublin in the summer of 1904. The main
characters are Stephen Dedalus (who appears in Joyce's
earlier, autobiographical *Portrait of the Artist as a Young
Man*), Leopold Bloom, a middle-aged Jewish advertisement
canvasser and his wife, Mollie. Joyce, for reasons difficult to
comprehend, based the structure of his novel on the *Odyssey*,
each main incident parodying or (sometimes very obliquely)
corresponding to an episode in Homer's epic. Apart from the
structural coherence that this procedure lends to *Ulysses* it
might also be a means of emphasizing the mythic, universal
elements he is attempting to convey; the invocation of the
Greek heroic myths both parallel and mock the squalor, the
comically unheroic events and characters of this
twentieth-century epic. Stephen Dedalus is a modern version
of Telemachus, Bloom is Ulysses and Mollie (or Marion) is
Penelope.

Bloom and Dedalus, the young poet, wander about the city of Dublin, meeting briefly at times then finally coming together for a longer period in a brothel from which Bloom takes the younger man to his home. The 'stream of consciousness' technique as employed by Joyce is wonderfully effective for, unlike Virginia Woolf, he is able to inhabit the minds and sensibilities, and indeed the bodies, of characters completely dissimilar both from himself and from each other. The famous soliloquy of Mrs Bloom with which this strange and marvellous novel ends is an uncannily authentic and moving demonstration of the workings of a particular woman's random thoughts and feelings as she lies in bed after making love and, furthermore, it succeeds in establishing Mollie as an archetypal, universal woman-figure.

If you should find *Ulysses* difficult to follow, and there can be no questioning that it is an imaginative work which makes more demands than most, you should nevertheless be able to derive enjoyment from individual scenes and from the magnificent surge and flow of the language. It is one of the very few novels that I find can be read purely for the verbal excitement it provides – though of course it offers far more than this alone – and like a major poem it can be picked up, opened at any page and tasted with delight. The technical innovations of *Ulysses* have influenced, directly or indirectly, every novelist of importance to emerge since its publication.

D. H. Lawrence

Joyce, the Jesuit-trained Irish scholar, steeped in the literature of the past and present, a man whose passionate obsession it was to create a new and great work of art, was an entirely different kind of writer from his great English contemporary, D. H. Lawrence (1885–1930), who was the son of a Nottinghamshire miner, brought up in the tradition of nonconformist religious dissent, a man burning with prophetic and rebellious zeal to change the world which he viewed as corrupted by a materialistic civilization that was crippling and blinding man's instinctive wisdom and joyous response to experience. Lawrence was not greatly concerned with the formal problems posed by the novel: true to his own beliefs in the wisdom of instinct and passion he wrote from the heart and senses with the result that his novels are generally lacking in structural control but they are all illuminated by brilliant passages of sensuous description and a remarkable gift for entering into the consciousness of his characters, both male and female.

Sons and Lovers (1913) is an autobiographical novel in which Lawrence analyses the relationship between his mother and father and traces his own development as a man and artist. Mrs Morel, the mother in the novel, is closely based upon Lawrence's own mother who was socially superior and better educated than her husband who, as Walter Morel, is presented by the author with much less sympathy than that extended to the woman. The details of the Midlands background are superbly captured and the emotional turmoils of the various principals communicated with sharp conviction, but the novel lacks not only the balance of a strong formal sense but the psychological balance of objectivity. The intensity of feeling, as so often in Lawrence, is conveyed by a monochromatic tone and it becomes, before the end of the book, oppressive. In his polemical writings and in some of his poems Lawrence showed a kind of humour, aggressive, even brutal but humour nonetheless, but this quality is usually absent from his novels, which are generally charged with the unrelenting earnestness of the obsessed visionary. At his best, in Women in Love (1920) for example, he often achieves an impressive physical power that is all his own, but his determination to preach a dubious gospel which asserts the value of primitive intuition and sensuality over reason and intelligence is finally reductive, and in Lady Chatterley's Lover (published in an expurgated edition in 1928 but not presented to the public in its original form until 1960 after a long and highly publicized legal battle) he can sink to embarrassing levels of bathos, especially in the grotesque conversation between Mellors, the gamekeeper, and Lady Chatterley's father.

satire and comedy

The stature of Lawrence and Joyce seems greater now than ever before and it tends to dwarf the significance of their

satire and
comedy

contemporaries and successors. Aldous Huxley (1894–1963) enjoyed a high reputation during the twenties and thirties with novels like *Crome Yellow* (1921), *Those Barren Leaves* (1925), *Point Counterpoint* (1928) and *Brave New World* (1932) but, though his books can be read today with interest and pleasure, he now seems to us a distinctly minor figure of his time. He is a novelist who is disgusted with a contemporary society which he regards as trivial and trivializing, philistine, greedy, unimaginative and soulless. His satire, however, is not sharply focused and the reader is aware that much of what he deplores is to be found in his own literary personality and attitudes. Far more successful as satirist and comic novelist is Evelyn Waugh (1903–1966), a writer whose satirical purposes coupled with the sheer funniness of his comedy have caused many academic literary critics to underestimate his exceptional talent for he is, to my mind, one of the very finest imaginative prose writers of the century.

Evelyn Waugh

Evelyn Waugh

In his early novels, *Decline and Fall* (1928), *Vile Bodies* (1930) and *Black Mischief* (1932) Waugh produced a kind of satirical comedy in which the comedy is far stronger than the satire. As satire these novels cannot really be counted entirely successful for Waugh feels more affection than loathing for his targets, the vapid, amoral 'bright young things' of the period. In *A Handful of Dust* (1934), however, a dark thread of genuine despair moves beneath the coruscating surface of comic invention. Tony Last has inherited a great Gothic country house, Hetton Abbey, in which each bedroom is named after a character from the Arthurian legends. The place symbolizes Tony's immaturely romantic nature, his impulse to retreat from the exigent and often vicious present to a dreamlike world of outmoded beliefs and values. His wife deceives him with an odious character called Beaver and when his little son is killed in a riding accident she apparently feels no grief but seizes the opportunity to divorce Tony. He, in a characteristically old-fashioned gesture, goes off to South America in search of a lost city and on his travels through the jungle he is captured by a weirdly sinister half-caste, Mr Todd, who keeps him prisoner, interminably reading the works of Charles Dickens to his crazed captor.

Some critics have taken the view that Waugh's best work is to be found in the earlier novels but, brilliantly funny though they are, his later books *Brideshead Revisited* (1945), *The Loved One* (1948), and the Second World War trilogy, *Men At Arms* (1952), *Officers and Gentlemen* (1955) and *Unconditional Surrender* (1961) show a steady deepening and strengthening of his formidable talents. Something of the youthful vitality and sparkle may have disappeared but the comedy is still richly satisfying, the structural control complete and, most importantly, the depth of psychological insight and sympathy greatly increased.

Anthony Powell

A writer who is sometimes compared with Waugh is Anthony Powell (b. 1905), but although they both deal with the same social milieu and period and could both broadly be classified as comic or satirical novelists, Powell's style and intentions are essentially different from Waugh's. His early novels, *Afternoon Men* (1931) and *From a View to a Death* (1933) are closest in tone to the social comedies of Waugh but even here one finds a weightier, less effervescent style and a greater reliance for effect on the comedy of character rather than situation and in his major work, the dozen separate novels which form the 'Music of Time' sequence, he emerges as an assiduous chronicler of a period of English history as experienced by a particular social group which is bound firmly together by shared education, cultural interests, family or emotional ties. The historical period covered is from the Depression years, the rise of Facism, the Spanish Civil War, through the Second World War to its aftermath, but the narrator, Nicholas Jenkins, refers to these events only insofar as they effect the private lives of the various people with whom he is involved. A fictional world is created in which the larger political dramas that provide front-page headlines are of significance mainly because they shake the kaleidoscope of the group's relationships into fresh patterns, and Powell is persuasive in showing that this world is closer to the one we all inhabit than the objective international one of the conventional historian. Whether 'The Music of Time' sequence will take its place among the major fictional achievements of the century is conjectural. It is an ambitious project and resourcefully carried out but Powell's prose style, aiming at dispassionate objectivity and judged appropriate to the rather negative and scholarly character of Jenkins, does become more and more sententious and excessively orotund as the novels succeed one another. There are moments of high comedy and the narrative keeps a steady grip on the reader's attention but I am less certain of the novels' secure place in our literature than I am of those of Waugh whose best work seems, like fine liquor, to improve with the passage of time.

the appeal of the modern novel

Of the novelists so far mentioned in this chapter James Joyce is the most secure in his reputation among academic critics but he is probably the least widely read by people who have no professional concern with literature. *Ulysses* is an indisputably great book but, because Joyce was breaking new ground and because of its extreme complexity, it is one which makes greater demands on its reader than more orthodox works of fiction and it is doubtful whether it will ever achieve the vast popularity of equally great novels like *David Copperfield* or Tolstoy's *War and Peace.* This does not mean, though, that the modern novel which appeals to a wide and not specially educated readership and which is written in a traditional form must be artistically inferior to experimental work. Evelyn Waugh's best novels are in my opinion as fine as any written in our century though they are stylistically and structurally quite uninnovatory and Waugh's friend and contemporary Graham Greene (b. 1904) has, almost from the start of his career, been immensely popular, though few critics would question the solid literary value of his best novels. His achievements in combining the narrative drive, the sheer readability of the most gripping novel of suspense with shrewd and subtle analysis of character and the mastery of traditional form and a style which has its own inimitable rhythm and tone, is one to admire and be grateful for.

Graham Greene

Greene is an immensely prolific author and everything he has written is at least readable though, as he has made clear by dividing his output into 'Entertainments' and 'Novels', some of his less ambitious stories are not to be judged by the same strict standard as the main works which include *England Made Me* (1935), *The Power and the Glory* (1940), *The Heart of the Matter* (1948) and *The End of the Affair* (1951), all of which seem to me to be important contributions to the literature of the twentieth century as well as absorbing and moving tales. Each of these books is set in a different part of the world, Scandinavia, Mexico, Africa and England and, while the physical background of Greene's novels is always conveyed vividly it is the same metaphysical world that is presented, a place where evil is ubiquitous and inerradicable and redemption is possible only through the sacrifice of worldly happiness. Where he excels is in his gift for presenting moral conflict, the endless opposition of good and evil, in the form of the thriller or adventure romance, providing penetrating insights into the sources of human behaviour. As a Roman Catholic he frequently ventures into spiritual territory in which he finds himself arriving at conclusions which verge upon doctrinal heresy and, in fact, some of his work has been officially condemned by the Church. Even the agnostic or sceptical reader may be disconcerted by his fascination with corruption which has led him to invest evil with a paradoxical glamour.

The religious, or the specifically Christian, preoccupations which provided the moral core of Greene's novels until the 1950s began, in the sixties, to give way to more general and political concerns and while he continued to produce admirable and enjoyable books they lack something of the intensity of the best of his earlier works.

postwar novelists

Among the other novelists who were building their reputa-
tions in the years following the end of the Second World War
there are few to rival Greene, either for readability or artistic
accomplishment, though Lawrence Durrell (b. 1912) achieved
wide popularity and provoked much critical debate with the
publication of his 'Alexandria Quartet' which consists of
Justine (1957), *Balthazar* (1958), *Mountolive* (1958) and *Clea*
(1960). In these novels the exotic background is richly evoked
and the same complex and tempestuous relationships are presented and examined from different viewpoints in each book.
Durrell writes with tremendous imaginative energy and
though the sensuous colouring and density of his prose can at
times be cloying he generally provides a corrective sharpness
of wit and observation which holds the reader captive.

William Golding

William Golding (b. 1911), whose first novel *Lord of the Flies*
(1954) commands a style of much greater austerity is still
developing his range as an artist though the concerns of even
his most recent work can be seen to be clearly related to his
earlier deep interest in – one might almost say obsession with
– human innocence and evil. *Lord of the Flies* is ironically
linked with the Victorian boys' adventure story *Coral Island*
by R. M. Ballantyne but in Golding's novel the boys on the
island do not show cheerful British resourcefulness and pluck
but rapidly degenerate to a state of superstitious barbarity. In
The Inheritors (1955) we are shown a world which has only
just evolved from the primeval animal state and Golding
succeeds in the immensely difficult task of entering into the
consciousness of a creature who is scarcely fully human. The
story is in essence a re-casting of the biblical Fall of Man, the
loss of innocence.

experimental vs traditional

The variety and breadth of the modern novel's scope had, by the end of the 1950s, become enormous. The techniques introduced and developed by James Joyce and Virginia Woolf had been absorbed and modified by writers who could then adapt these methods for their own needs. Broadly speaking, serious fiction could be divided into two camps, the deliberately experimental and the essentially traditional, but there was, and still continues to be, considerable overlapping of these types. Perhaps a more accurate distinction could be made between those novels, the aims of which are fundamentally poetic, and those whose primary concern is with narrative, character and ideas; the first kind, of which Virginia Woolf's *The Waves* and James Joyce's *Ulysses* are examples, are concerned chiefly with language, its radiance, glitter, magic and music: action and character are important but principally because they require the inventive play of language for their realization and development. The second kind – Arnold Bennett's *The Old Wives' Tale* or E. M. Forster's *A Passage to India* will serve as types – are primarily aiming at giving dramatic and coherent expression to certain ideas about man and his relation to society and the universe or simply to telling a story which may illustrate the irony, bitterness and glory of human existence: language is important but it is subservient to the author's first aim; it is a means to an end. In the 'poetic' novels – as in poetry itself – the dance of language comes close to being an end in itself. In the most rewarding novels it seems to me that a middle ground is occupied between these two polarities; in the best work of Dickens, for instance, it is impossible to separate event and its expression: the incident, character or scene will assume a haunting power to root itself in the memory long after the book has been put aside and this power is at least as much a consequence of the language which embodies the action as it is of the dramatic nature of the event. This fusion of poetic intensity and narrative energy and invention is found in the best of Graham Greene and Evelyn Waugh and very powerfully in a novel called *Under the Volcano* by Malcolm Lowry (1909–1957).

**experimental
vs
traditional**

Malcolm Lowry

Malcolm Lowry published a short autobiographical novel, *Ultramarine,* in 1933 and a collection of stories and fragments appeared after his death, but he was really a one-book man and that book was *Under the Volcano* (1947). He spent most of his life abroad, mainly in various parts of North America and Mexico, and he became at an early age an incurable alcoholic. The central character of *Under the Volcano* is an alcoholic, but the novel is not autobiographical in the sense of being a fictionalized account of Lowry's own experiences, though it could not have been written by anyone who had no first hand knowledge of the surreal torments and exultations of dipso-mania and the events take place against a superbly realized backcloth of the Mexico he knew so well. It is a tragic story of a man of honour and some nobility being humiliated and destroyed by his addiction to drink but it is written with such sympathy and in language of such richness and power that its total effect is, paradoxically, one of splendour rather than negation and, despite its darkness of mood, it is continuously illuminated by flashes of wit and pure comedy which provide the necessary balance that distinguishes major art.

foreign influences

Among the many influences that have worked upon the British novel in the first fifty odd years of this century – the effects of two global wars, advances in psychological theories of behaviour, scientific or quasi-scientific enquiries into the nature of time, the formal influence of the cinema (flashbacks, rapid cuts, dissolves and close-ups etc. have been absorbed into the novelist's techniques), radio and television, greater freedom of travel – we must not overlook the importance of the fiction of other countries. Developments in the French novel have always been noted and, where useful, absorbed by English writers, but with more and more translations of the literature of other nations being published – South America, Japan, China, Germany, Israel, Russia – the more experimental British novelists have become, though rather

cautiously, less insular in their formal and stylistic methods. **foreign**
The fiction from overseas which has been, for obvious **influences**
linguistic reasons, the most available and potentially the most
likely to provide stimulus and suggest new directions for
British novelists is that of North America, which developed its
individual identity and produced a number of massively
influential and exciting individual works in the first half of the
century. The next chapter will be devoted to the most gifted
and historically important of these authors who established
the American novel and, indeed, the American language as
something quite different from the slightly disreputable
relation of this island's literature and tongue which it had
been previously regarded as by most Britons and many
Americans.

7

THE AMERICAN NOVEL 1900–1960

The coming-of-age of the American novel in the present century as a national art-form which could at least hold its own with the fiction of any other country in the world was celebrated by an enormous proliferation of novels, too many to be treated in detail here. However, the emergence in the 1920s of three American novelists of exceptional genius makes my task more manageable. An appreciation and understanding of the work of this trio should lead inevitably, through an acquaintance with the lesser though formidably gifted writers whose work has directly or indirectly been influenced by them, to a comprehensive view of the American novel in the first half-dozen decades of this century. The three key-figures are Ernest Hemingway (1898–1961), F. Scott Fitzgerald (1896–1940), and William Faulkner (1897–1962).

Ernest Hemingway

Ernest Hemingway Since Hemingway's death by suicide his reputation among academic critics seems to have faded a little, though the adverse judgements passed on his work are invariably tempered by an awareness of his potent and lasting influence on the prose-style of virtually every succeeding novelist writing in English and on a number of foreign authors. Objections to certain weaknesses in his novels can quite easily be justified. He has been accused of a crude over-simplification of human – especially masculine – values. Physical courage, loyalty and honesty are, for him, far more admirable than intellect, sensitivity and imagination. Bull-fighting, big-game hunting and fishing are more ennobling in our corrupt civilization than the practice of the arts, religion and philosophy. His heroes are tough stoical hunters or fighters, embodiments of primitive virtues, or cynical hedonists who despise the falsity and inhumanity of the society they have inherited. But, paradoxically, it is as an artist that he triumphs.

Ernest Hemingway

He was born in Illinois and, as a boy, he greatly enjoyed hunting and fishing in Northern Michigan, experiences which he drew upon for many of his magnificent short stories. After working briefly as a newspaper reporter in Kansas City he joined a volunteer ambulance unit in France and then transferred to the Italian Infantry with whom he fought until the end of the First World War, after which he lived in Paris among the raffish artists, writers and eccentrics who formed a colony of expatriate bohemians which included Ford Madox Ford, Scott Fitzgerald and Gertrude Stein. It was in this period that Hemingway applied himself to the business of training to become a great original artist, and Gertrude Stein played an important part in his education.

Gertrude Stein (1874–1946) was born in Pennsylvania and, after studying psychology and the anatomy of the brain at Johns Hopkins University, she left the US to settle in France and devote herself to writing, theorizing about literature in particular and the arts in general and maintaining a *salon* where avant-garde painters, poets, sculptors, and prose-writers regularly met. Her own experimental writing in verse and prose, her attempts to manufacture a prose-style which could create a cinematic effect of flowing continuity, are not likely to offer anyone except the researcher much pleasure, but, whatever her standing as a creative artist, the fact remains that she exercised a decisive influence over the

**Ernest
Hemingway**

writing of Hemingway and his forging of a style which has remained a model and inspiration to prose-writers of many kinds during the past half-century. This style, the principal features of which are a rigorous elimination of all decorative verbiage, a concentration of the power of the verb and noun, an almost primitive simplification of syntax and the subtle use of repeated words and rhythms, is powerfully effective for describing scenes of physical action and sensory experience though less able to deal with reflection and ambiguous mental or emotional processes. It has been crudely adopted by many American writers of adventure and crime fiction including Dashiel Hammett and Raymond Chandler, and its more subtle elements have been influential on the work of 'straight' novelists like John O'Hara (*Appointment in Samarra*) and *Butterfield 8*), Alfred Hayes (*The Girl on the Via Flaminia* and *In Love*), John Hersey (*A Bell for Adano* and *The War Lover*) and, as the author has publicly acknowledged, a writer so superficially different as Graham Greene.

Hemingway published a few short stories during his Paris sojourn and in these his main preoccupations expressed in that unique style which could combine a plain, muscular precision with an oddly haunting lyricism, were already being displayed. His first novel, *The Torrents of Spring* (1926), was a slight, satirical work which parodied the manner of Sherwood Anderson (1876–1941), a writer whom Hemingway admired and from whom he had learnt, but it was his second novel, *The Sun Also Rises* (1926) published in England under the title *Fiesta*, that established him as a new and dazzlingly original force on the contemporary literary scene.

Fiesta (I shall refer to it by its British title) still, after over half a century, carries much of its power to thrill, entertain and move the reader, and the passage of the years has deepened its mythological power to represent the spirit of a particular generation in a particular time and place. The time was the period immediately following the end of World War I and the place was Paris, though some of the action takes place in Spain. The characters are all young in years but, in various ways, scarred and embittered by the War and the collapse of the moral values which had seemed so securely established in pre-war Western civilization.

The central female character is Lady Brett Ashley, a young and beautiful English woman who is living on the Continent while she waits for a divorce after which she intends, though with no passionate eagerness, to marry the amiable but rather fatuous Michael Campbell. Her circle of Paris friends includes the narrator, Jake Barnes, an American newspaper correspondent whose war-wound has left him sexually impotent. He is the man whom Brett truly loves, though one wonders whether his emasculation, which renders fulfilment impossible, is not a cause of this 'love', in which case Brett's passion is perverse, if not perverted. Others in the Paris expatriate circle are Bill Gorton, Jake's close friend, and Robert Cohn, an American Jewish novelist who falls in love with Brett and is treated by her with cruelty.

Ernest Hemingway

The principal characters leave Paris for a trip to Spain where they visit the fiesta at Pamplona and attend the bullfights. Brett is violently attracted to a young bullfighter, Pedro Romero, and leaves her fiancé to live with him, but the relationship is short-lived and she returns to the easy-going Michael who she knows will tolerate her caprices and make few demands, or even criticisms of her character.

Brett Ashley is a bitch and it is one of the flaws in the novel that Hemingway does not seem to realize what a monster he has created. His treatment of Cohn, too, reveals a streak of anti-Semitism of which the author seems to be unconscious but where the book triumphs is in its evocation of the excitement of the Spanish bullring, the Paris of the twenties and the sense of a world which has lost its moral bearings. And, especially in the Spanish scenes, Hemingway shows a gift for conveying the physical reality of simple sensory experience, the pleasures of food and wine and bodily exertion and repose. Here is an example of his mastery of a descriptive prose which physically involves the reader in what is happening instead of merely presenting a sequence of verbal pictures:

> I got my rod that was leaning against the tree, took the bait can and landing-net, and walked out on to the dam. It was built to provide a head of water for driving logs. The gate was up, and I sat on one of the squared timbers and watched the smooth apron of water

Ernest
Hemingway

before the river tumbled into the falls. In the white water at the foot of the dam it was deep. As I baited up, a trout shot up out of the white water into the falls and was carried down. Before I could finish baiting, another trout jumped at the falls, making the same lovely arc and disappearing into the water that was thundering down. I put on a good-sized sinker and dropped into the white water close to the edge of the timbers of the dam.

I did not feel the first trout strike. When I started to pull up I felt that I had one and brought him, fighting and bending the rod almost double, out of the boiling water at the foot of the falls, and swung him up and on to the dam. He was a good trout, and I banged his head against the timber so that he quivered out straight, and then slipped him into my bag.

While I had him on, several trout had jumped at the falls. As soon as I baited up and dropped in again I hooked another and brought him in the same way. In a little while I had six. They were all about the same size. I laid them out, side by side, all their heads point-ing the same way, and looked at them. They were beautifully coloured and firm and hard from the cold water. It was a hot day, so I slit them all and shucked out the insides, gills and all, and tossed them over across the river. I took the trout ashore, washed them in the cold, smoothly heavy water above the dam, and then picked some ferns and packed them all in the bag, three trout on a layer of ferns, then another layer of ferns, then three more trout, and then covered them with ferns.

They looked nice in the ferns, and now the bag was bulky, and I put it in the shade of the tree.

It was very hot on the dam, so I put my worm-can in the shade with the bag, and got a book out of the pack and settled down under the tree to read until Bill should come up for lunch.

This command of an individual prose-style which could almost magically draw the reader into the physical world depicted in the novel was again used to impressive effect in Hemingway's next and perhaps most famous book, *A Farewell to Arms* (1929). It is a love story of great tenderness and at the same time one of the finest war novels ever to be

written. The hero, Frederic Henry, is an American lieutenant
serving in an Italian ambulance unit during the First World
War. He falls in love with an English nurse, Catherine
Barkley, and after he is wounded and taken to a military
hospital in Milan she is able to join him in her professional
capacity and a passionate affair develops. Catherine becomes
pregnant and Henry is returned to duty but he deserts in order
to rejoin her and together they flee to Switzerland. The end is
tragic and Hemingway handles the writing of it with a
reticence and understatement which increases its poignancy.

**Ernest
Hemingway**

In this short extract from the scene where Henry is
wounded in a German bombardment we can see how brilliantly the physical experience is communicated. Hemingway
does not merely describe; he causes the events to happen.
The reader is involved in a way which is, quite literally,
physical. If you read the first four sentences aloud you will find
that the pacing of them, the deliberate lack of comma-pauses,
the repetitions of '. . .out of myself and out and out and out. . .'
will actually cause breathlessness and the last very short sentence comes as a physical relief:

> Through the other noise I heard a cough, then came
> the chuh-chuh-chuh-chuh then there was flash, as a
> blast-furnace door is swung open, and a roar that
> started white and went red and on and on in a rushing
> wind. I tried to breathe but my breath would not come
> and I felt myself rush bodily out of myself and out and
> out and out and all the time bodily in the wind. I went
> out swiftly, all of myself and I knew I was dead and
> that it had all been a mistake to think you just died.
> Then I floated, and instead of going on felt myself
> slide back. I breathed and I was back. The ground was
> torn up and in front of my head there was a splintered
> beam of wood. In the jolt of my head I heard somebody
> crying. I thought somebody was screaming. I tried to
> move but I could not move. I heard the machine-guns
> and rifles firing across the river and all along the river.
> There was a great splashing and I saw the star-shells
> go up and burst and float whitely and rockets going up
> and heard the bombs, all this in a moment and then I
> heard close to me someone saying, 'Mamma mia! Oh,
> mamma mia!' I pulled and twisted and got my legs

**Ernest
Hemingway**

loose finally and turned round and touched him. It was Passini and when I touched him he screamed. His legs were toward me and I saw in the dark and the light that they were both smashed above the knee. One leg was gone and the other was held by tendons and part of the trouser and the stump twitched and jerked as though it were not connected. He bit his arm and moaned, 'Oh, mamma mia, mamma mia,' then, 'Dio ti salvi, Maria. Dio ti salvi, Maria. Oh Jesus shoot me Christ shoot me, Mamma mia, Mamma mia, oh purest lovely Mary shoot me. Stop it. Stop it. Stop it. Oh Jesus lovely Mary stop it. Oh oh oh oh,' then choking, 'Mamma mamma mia.' Then he was quiet, biting his arm, the stump of his leg twitching.

After *A Farewell to Arms* Hemingway's novels declined in quality, though *To Have and Have Not* (1937), which has been adversely judged by some critics, seems to me a fine story of one man's fight against insuperable odds and one which works, too, as an allegory of the individual's tragic fate in an increasingly heartless and totalitarian society. Nevertheless there can be no denying that *For Whom the Bell Tolls* (1940), his longest novel, contains flaws of sentimentality and weakness of characterization which must disqualify it from any claim to greatness and *The Old Man and the Sea* (1952), which has received great critical praise, seems to me an essentially false work in which Hemingway comes close to parodying himself. His most flawless writing is to be found in the short stories which seem to escape the deterioration which afflicted the later novels and are among the very finest prose works of the imagination to be found in the literature of the English Language.

F. Scott Fitzgerald

**F. Scott
Fitzgerald**

Hemingway's relationship with Scott Fitzgerald when they knew each other in Paris in the middle and later 1920s was marked by mutual admiration for each other's work, though Hemingway's account of the friendship, recorded in his book of memoirs, *A Moveable Feast* (1964), is marred by a note of slightly bullying patronage. Both as writers and as men they were very different types, sharing only a deeply serious devotion to their art. Where Hemingway was a tough, belligerent character who enjoyed such violent pastimes as hunting, bullfighting and boxing (his performances in the ring become less impressive when we discover that his opponents were fighters of the calibre of Ezra Pound and T. S. Eliot), Fitzgerald was a sensitive, gentle person whose few exhibitions of unruly behaviour were the consequence of too much alcohol.

Scott Fitzgerald was born in St Paul, Minnesota, and, after studying at Princeton, he joined the Army in 1917 but spent his military service in the United States. While in training-camps he wrote the first draft of his novel, *This Side of Paradise,* and the revised manuscript was published in 1920. It was very successful and it proved to be the first step in establishing Fitzgerald as, not merely the spokesman but almost the embodiment of the 'Jazz Age', that febrile period of American history when the disillusionment of the post-war young found its expression in self-destructive hedonism. His second novel, *The Beautiful and the Damned* (1922), a slight but readable work, dealt superficially with the inevitable corruption of wealth and living for transitory pleasure alone, but nothing he had so far written could have prepared the reading public for *The Great Gatsby* (1925).

This novel is one of the glories of American literature. It is not a novel conceived on the grand scale but within its comparatively brief scope it contains a wealth of allegorical significance. And it is written with exemplary economy in a beautiful clean prose, the rhythms of which haunt the consciousness of the reader like the cadences of great poetry. *The Great Gatsby* is a fable of the doomed romantic dream which can never materialize and, in the figure of Jay Gatsby, we can see America itself, unscrupulous in its quest for power but divided in its heart by an irreconcilable hunger for nobility and purity. But if these comments should give the impression that the novel is in any way pretentious or that it contains passages of philosophical speculation I must stress at once that this is not the case and that it is a continuously exciting story.

It is told by Nick Carraway, a young bonds salesman

**F. Scott
Fitzgerald**

who lives in West Egg, Long Island. His home overlooks a
great mansion set in splendid grounds, occupied by the
mysterious figure of Jay Gatsby. Gatsby, whose social origins
were very humble, had nevertheless been commissioned
during the war and as a young lieutenant he had met Nick's
cousin, Daisy, and fallen in love with her and his acquisition of
vast wealth (all gained, it transpires, by criminal means) and
his extravagant displays of it have the single aim of impress-
ing Daisy who has married Tom Buchanan, a wealthy and
brutally stupid representative of the upper classes. Gatsby
succeeds in meeting Daisy again and she succumbs to his
devoted attentions. Her husband has a casual sexual relationship with Myrtle Wilson, the cheaply sensual wife of an
older and pathetic small garage-owner. Events move to an
ironically tragic climax of violent death. Myrtle is locked in
her room by her jealous husband but she escapes and, running on to the highway, she is knocked down and killed by a
car driven by Daisy. Gatsby, the personification of quixotic
chivalry, tries to protect Daisy, and Buchanan, motivated by
jealousy, seeks out Wilson and tells him that it was Gatsby
who killed Myrtle. The garage-owner shoots Gatsby and then
turns the gun on himself. Gatsby's dream ends in nightmare.
Only the spoiled darlings of social privilege – Daisy and Tom
Buchanan – escape unharmed.

The Great Gatsby is as close to a flawless novel as any
I have read and it is one which can be returned to repeatedly
with ever-increasing pleasure. Fitzgerald's fortunes declined
after the publication of his best novel. His beautiful but un-
stable wife, Zelda, suffered a breakdown and was expensively
hospitalized and, finally, Fitzgerald was forced through shor-
tage of money to undertake film-writing in Hollywood. He
was drinking heavily and expending too much time and
energy on the accomplished but minor short stories that he
wrote for a quick cash return. But he continued to work at his
next novel, *Tender is the Night* (1934), constantly re-writing
parts which he felt were unsatisfactory, and when it was published he was deeply depressed by its cool critical reception.

Tender is the Night is a much longer and more
complex work than *The Great Gatsby* and it must be acknowledged that it is not a completely successful one. In *Gatsby*

Fitzgerald succeeded, as completely as any other novelist of the century, in distancing himself from his own preoccupations and objectifying them in a work of art which, though profoundly moving, possesses a classical perfection of structure and style. *Tender is the Night* is a subjective, romantic work: the author himself, in the fairly transparent guise of Dick Diver, a psychiatrist, is at the centre of the book and most of the other characters have their identifiable counterparts in Fitzgerald's life. The story deals with Diver's rise to professional eminence, social and financial success, his marriage to the beautiful Nicole who is his patient as well as wife and mother of his two children, and it traces the gradual decline of their mutual love into suspicion, resentment and final betrayal. Diver, the gifted, attractive and charming success degenerates into a wretched drink-sodden failure.

The novel is rich in splendidly realized scenes and precisely observed characters, but something of its central character's despair infects the later pages and a note of self-pity and impotence in the face of adversity reduces what might have been tragedy to the level of pathos. Nevertheless *Tender is the Night* is a considerable achievement, a novel which, despite its imperfections, possesses the power to haunt the imagination in a way that only major writing can, and, though it is too personal and localized to serve, as its author would have wished, as a symbol of the sickness of twentieth-century life, it does succeed in poignantly expressing the disillusionment of the American post-war generation of the talented young.

Scott Fitzgerald fought courageously to overcome his addiction to alcohol, to support his sick wife and educate their daughter, working at the thankless grind of film-writing. His last novel, which was unfinished at the time of his death but was near enough to completion to be published in 1941, is a perceptive study of a movie mogul and the Hollywood milieu, its heartlessness, hypocrisy and essential corruption. It shows something of the objective precision of *The Great Gatsby* but is more sardonic in tone, deliberately eliminating the elegiac lyricism which runs through his masterpiece, and it was the first of a number of distinguished Hollywood novels by other authors, including Budd Schulberg's *What Makes Sammy Run*

F. Scott
Fitzgerald

(1941), Norman Mailer's *The Deer Park* (1955) and by far the most impressive of these, Nathanael West's *The Day of the Locust* (1939).

William Faulkner

William
Faulkner

Fitzgerald and Hemingway were both artists who exercised considerable influence over succeeding novelists, especially Hemingway, whose stylistic innovations presented a model for writers whose primary concern was to present the realities of physical sensation, but neither was an 'experimental' novelist in the structural sense; each was content to follow established tradition in the unfolding of narrative and presentation of dialogue. William Faulkner was not a theoretical experimentalist deliberately seeking to extend the formal possibilities of his medium, but in the process of expressing his vision of the world he found that the traditional narrative means were insufficient and he developed a style and structural procedure that was different from anything else in American fiction though having something in common with the methods of Virginia Woolf and James Joyce.

Faulkner's first novel, *Soldiers' Pay* (1926) was fairly conventional in form, owing something to Sherwood Anderson, but with the publication of *Sartoris* (1929) he began the great saga of Yoknapatawpha County (an imagined setting in northern Mississippi) and the people who lived there, the Compson, Sartoris, and Benbow families, who represented the Old South, and the Snopeses, an unscrupulous and vicious tribe, who displace them. In a series of novels Faulkner dissects the life of the region from the pre-Civil War period to the modern age, but in doing this he is concerned with far more than the historical and social changes which take place. He uses the territory and its history as a dramatic metaphor for the universal and eternal struggle between good and evil and his prose is charged with a density and power which is peculiarly his own. He makes use of the 'stream of consciousness' technique but in a manner and for purposes essentially different from those of Virginia Woolf and James Joyce.

In *The Sound and the Fury* (1929), to me his most
remarkable novel, and the one in which he introduces the
Compson family, the narrative is unfolded in four parts, three
of them through the stream of consciousness of Benjy,
Quentin and Jason Compson and the fourth as an objective
narration. Benjy is a 33-year-old idiot incapable of speech and
the way in which Faulkner reveals the tragic history of the
family through the fragmented images and memories which
are awakened in his mind by vagrant sensuous stimuli is
accomplished with a mastery that is almost miraculous. The
novel is moving, violent and at times funny, and the language,
its flowing rhythms and richness of sound and colouring,
possesses the magical, incantatory quality of great poetry.

Faulkner's major work is to be found in the seven
novels he published between 1929 and 1936 which include
the splendid *Sartoris* (1929), *Light in August* (1932) and
Absalom, Absalom! (1936) but perhaps his most widely read
novel is *Sanctuary* which has acquired an ambiguous
reputation, partly because of its sensational subject-matter
and partly because Faulkner claimed that he wrote it cynically
to make money. Later he denied that this was his motive in
writing the book and, whatever the author's motivation may
have been, it is a formidable piece of work, a novel which is
permeated with the sense of evil, a nightmare of violence
where almost all of the principal characters seem to be the
puppets of their passions, greed, lust and avarice. *Sanctuary* is
a shocker, yet Faulkner's irony and wit, the prodigal
inventiveness and ability to create utterly convincing
characters, however monstrous, insist on its being taken
seriously.

The story deals with an 18-year-old college girl,
Temple Drake, who is out with a young man who has drunk
too much. He wrecks the car on a lonely road and they make
their way to an isolated house, seeking help, only to find that
the place is occupied by a gang of vicious criminals whose
chief is Popeye, a retarded psychopath. Temple's escort is
beaten up and he, exhibiting a strong instinct for self-
preservation at any cost, escapes, leaving the girl to be
molested and finally raped – though in a horrifically artificial
way – by Popeye. She is next placed in a brothel in Memphis

**William
Faulkner**

and after various killings, a lynching and Popeye's execution she is returned to her father who takes her away to Paris.

This crude outline of some of the chief events will give an entirely false impression of the quality of the book. It is a horrifying novel but the writing is that of a master and there are scenes which stay indelibly in the mind. It is Faulkner's most pessimistic work, one in which there seems to be little hope for humanity, and here it is uncharacteristic, for however tragic the tone and vision of his major novels there is always present a sense of the essential strength, courage and latent nobility of the human spirit. When he received the Nobel Prize for Literature in 1950 he ended his Speech of Acceptance with these words:

> It is easy enough to say that man is immortal simply because he will endure: that when the last ding-dong of doom has clanged and faded from the last worthless rock hanging tideless in the last red and dying evening, that even then there will still be one more sound: that of his puny, inexhaustible voice, still talking. I refuse to accept this. I believe that man will not merely endure: he will prevail. He is immortal, not because he alone among creatures has an inexhaustible voice, but because he has a soul, a spirit capable of compassion and sacrifice and endurance. The poet's, the writer's, duty is to write about these things. It is his privilege to help man endure by lifting his heart, by reminding him of the courage and honour and hope and pride and compassion and pity and sacrifice which have been the glory of his past. The poet's voice need not merely be the record of man, it can be one of the props, the pillars to help him endure and prevail.

It is the 'spirit capable of compassion and sacrifice and endurance' which informs the best work of Faulkner and invests it with tragic grandeur.

Southern school

Faulkner's mythologizing of the American South, and his profound and poetic explorations of the darkness of inherited evil and the combative brightness of the will to survive and create, exercised a great deal of influence on the American novel. A

school of Southern writing emerged which included such
excellent novelists as Robert Penn Warren (b. 1905), Eudora Welty (b. 1909), Carson McCullers (b. 1917), Flannery O'Connor (1925–1964) and William Styron (b. 1925), each with his or her individual style and preoccupations but all indebted to Faulkner.

The stylistic innovations of Hemingway have served as a model for almost every novelist of note now writing in the English or American language, and Fitzgerald produced, in *The Great Gatsby,* a work of fiction which must be as near to faultless as human capabilities can approach. But the towering stature of these giants of the twentieth-century American novel by no means completely overshadowed the achievements of their most accomplished contemporaries and successors. Indeed during the second and third quarters of this century the scope, variety and profusion of American fiction has to some extent asserted its ascendancy over the British novel, which many readers and critics have regarded as comparatively tame, small-scale and provincial.

Jewish novelists

Nathanael West (1903–1940), one of the harbingers of the
great efflorescence of Jewish prose fiction which was to dominate the American literary scene after the Second World War, was not, during his brief life-time, accorded anything like the recognition he deserved but he is now generally reckoned to be among the most original novelists of the first half of the century. Even so, his most appreciative critics have not found him an easy author to classify. His two best works are the very short novels, *Miss Lonelyhearts* (1933) and *The Day of the Locust* (1939), the first a bitter and melancholy yet frequently funny story about a newspaper reporter who takes over the 'agony column' of his paper and becomes obsessed with the tragic-comic sufferings of his correspondents; the second, a ferocious satire on Hollywood, the shoddiness, cynicism and absurdity of the film-world. In both of these works West uses some of the means of communication that he is satirizing to create strange, surrealistic effects: in *Miss Lonelyhearts* the method of narration and presentation of

**Jewish
novelists**

characters has something of the deliberate harshness of outline and fracturing of continuity that is shown by the popular
newspaper comic-strip and many of the scenes in *The Day of
the Locust* possess the fluidity, the visual stridency of film,
especially the early black-and-white cinema.

Among the Jewish novelists who came after West and
have gained a literary eminence infinitely greater than that of
any other ethnic or religious group – including the Anglo-
Saxon Protestant – were Bernard Malamud (b. 1914), Saul
Bellow (b. 1915), J. D. Salinger (b. 1919) and Norman Mailer
(b. 1923). Malamud and Bellow are, I think, writers of far
greater accomplishment than Salinger and Mailer, though the
latter two have perhaps enjoyed greater popular recognition
or – in the case of Mailer – notoriety. This is not to say that
Mailer is not a novelist who possesses unusual gifts; rather
that these gifts are not always exercised under the necessary
restraints of art and are too frequently used or misused for the
most blatant kind of egotistical exhibitionism.

The Catcher in the Rye

**The Catcher
in the
Rye**

J. D. Salinger's first novel, *The Catcher in the Rye* (1951) is still
his most famous and I should say by far his best book. Its hero
is Holden Caulfield, a sixteen-year-old boy who, expelled
from his expensive school, embarks on a series of adventures
in New York. The story is told in the racy vernacular of the
time and place by Holden himself and it is, in parts, very
funny and, in others, quite moving. The technique and the
author's central preoccupation with innocence in a corrupt
world are strongly reminiscent of Huckleberry Finn and the
novel might reasonably be described as an up-dated, metro-
politan version of Mark Twain's classic. The sentimentality
which was kept by Salinger's wit and comic invention from
fatally injuring *The Catcher in the Rye* became more dominant
in his subsequent work and this weakness, allied to a rather
sickly form of religious mysticism, has by now disappointed all
of the hopes created by his first novel.

A streak of the meretricious, the flashily fake, which,
in quite different ways, runs through the work of both Mailer

and Salinger is absent from Malamud's solidly constructed, genuinely brilliant novels. His first, *The Natural*, deals satirically with the deep need for heroes which is always to be found in unheroic urban civilizations. The chief character is Roy Hobbs, a baseball player whose egotism and narcissism finally destroy him, not only professionally but as a human being. It is a savagely funny book but its purpose is very serious, for Malamud is exploring the problem of how much and in what way a man can learn from experience and suffering. His next two novels, *The Assistant* (1957) and *A New Life* (1961) are both, in their very different ways, concerned with the same problem, and both are highly readable, beautifully written pieces of work.

The Catcher in the Rye

Saul Bellow

Saul Bellow, who won the Nobel Prize for Literature in 1976, is generally regarded on both sides of the Atlantic as one of America's finest prose writers. His earliest two novels were *Dangling Man* (1944) and *The Victim* (1947), the first a short allegorical story of a young man waiting to be drafted into the army and meanwhile living in a curious state of suspended animation and the second, a painful study of the relations between Gentile and Jew. Then came *The Adventures of Augie March* (1947) in which Bellow moved away from the classic economy of his first two novels and produced a large-scale, picaresque story of a young Chicago Jew who experiences a series of adventures, some of which are of dangerous illegality, including robbery and the smuggling of immigrants over the Canadian border, before he finally, if precariously – for his is a world without dependable stability – settles down to marriage.

Saul Bellow

Augie March is a continuously engaging and very often funny novel but Bellow has interesting and quite profound philosophical preoccupations to explore and develop. Like his next novel, *Henderson the Rain King* (1959), it is much concerned with the search for personal identity and with the problem of self-realization through action. Augie's elder brother, Simon, chooses to conform to the expectations

Saul Bellow   of materialistic convention and, in pursuit of worldly success, becomes de-humanized. The younger brother, George, is mentally retarded and he retreats from reality to the protective emptiness of institutionalized existence. He is gentle, entirely without cruelty or acquisitiveness, but his virtue is negative. When Augie visits him in the asylum and takes him out for a walk George shrinks from the threatening realities of the everyday world and wishes only to be safely back in the asylum.

Catch 22

Catch 22   The search for identity, for the possibility of independent choice, the assertion of individuality in an increasingly mechanistic society is a common preoccupation in American fiction after the Second World War and in Joseph Heller's *Catch 22* (1961) it found memorable expression. This novel is often referred to as an anti-war satire; certainly the action takes place during the war against fascism and the setting is a US Air Force camp in Italy with excursions to Rome under allied occupation, and undoubtedly the cruel absurdity of modern war is pilloried. But Heller is doing more than condemning a particular historic event or an exceptional set of circumstances. The military life in which the individual is reduced to a number, where life and death are statistics, and behaviour which, in a more reasonable place and time, would be considered insane is now praised and rewarded is an extension of ordinary life in American society.

   Catch 22 is a wickedly funny and, at the same time, a deeply disturbing book. In it all of the traditional military virtues of courage, honour, obedience and loyalty are ridiculed and those who subscribe to them are shown as dupes or cynical exploiters of the gullible. The primary aim of the military machine, and by implication the aim of American society, is to rob the individual of all sense of identity so that he may be manipulated unresistingly in the way that faceless, heartless 'authority' decides. The true hero, Heller suggests, is the man who refuses to be manipulated, who regards his life as more valuable than any abstract principle. So Yossarian, the hero or anti-hero of *Catch 22*, has only one aim as member of the US Air Force, and that is to stay alive. Beneath the surface of comedy and surrealistic nightmare and farce there runs through this novel a vein of desperation, a sense that man has lost control of his destiny. The curiously dreamlike quality of so many of the sequences suggests too that reality and fantasy or dream are becoming more and more difficult to separate. One of the characters called Hungry Joe has a recurrent nightmare of a cat sleeping on his face. Finally he dies in his sleep and when his body is discovered a cat is indeed asleep on his face.

Catch 22

nightmare and reality

This satirical interweaving of nightmare and reality in presenting mid-twentieth-century American life is found in a number of novels of the fifties and sixties including excellent work by James Purdy, Thomas Pynchon and Kurt Vonnegut Jnr, though strangely enough the most accomplished practitioner of the mode and the writer who could probably claim to have initiated the style of dandified elegance which most effectively handles it was not a native American but a Russian who became a US citizen in 1945. Vladimir Nabokov (1899–1977) was born in St Petersburg but, as a refugee from the Revolution, he and his family came to England where he attended Trinity College, Cambridge, graduating in 1922. Between 1925 and 1940 he lived in Germany and France and wrote a number of poems and eight novels in Russian. In 1940 he settled in the United States and began to produce the novels in the English language by which he is best known.

**nightmare
and
reality**

Nabokov

Nabokov is in some respects an even more extraordinary literary phenomenon than Conrad for, unlike the Pole, he gained eminence as a writer in his native tongue before he turned to the English language in which he produced fiction, some of which must rank with the very finest of its time and

Nabokov

Nabokov genre. *Lolita,* his most famous book, was published in Paris in 1955, in America in 1958 and in Britain in 1959, and perhaps some explanation should be given for its rather unusually staggered presentation to the reading public. When the novel was completed in the fifties the 'moral' climate in regard to the publication of literature which dealt with sexual relationships – especially those which were in some way unconventional or 'aberrant' – was, by later standards, illiberal and *Lolita* was thought to be an indecent if not pornographic work. When we consider the almost absolute freedom of expression granted to writers today Nabokov's novel seems fairly innocuous; verbally it is unusually chaste in that no use is made of the formerly taboo Anglo-Saxon monosyllables, the use of which seems almost obligatory in novels published since the Lady Chatterley case. The caution shown by American and British publishers over bringing out *Lolita* was provoked by its subject-matter, for Nabokov was writing about a mature man's passionate physical obsession with a twelve-year-old girl, a theme which was bound to dismay self-appointed guardians of public morality.

Lolita is an erotic novel but it could be labelled 'obscene' only by those who regard sexual passion as inherently vile. It is in fact a black comedy, a brilliant exploration of an aspect of obsessive physical desire which is generally ignored – the element of absurdity. But it is also a powerful evocation of the obsession as experienced by the central character, Humbert Humbert. Nabokov has suggested that the novel is an account of his 'love affair with the English language' and other commentators on the book have seen its heroine, Lolita, as America itself, young (in contrast to the wise but corrupt European, Humbert Humbert), predatory, shallow, irresistibly appealing, but doomed to an early corpulent dullness. Nabokov's own account is persuasive for the language throughout the book is rhythmically beguiling, visually glittering and lyrically precise. Perhaps it is lacking in the warmth of human sympathy, and this objection can be levelled at all of Nabokov's fiction, but it is a dazzling achievement and one which, as we shall see in the next chapter, continues to influence the development of the novel in both America and Great Britain.

8

THE NOVEL NOW

is the novel dying?

During the past three decades the question 'Is the novel a dying literary form?' has been asked periodically by academic commentators on social and cultural matters and by literary journalists and other media-men. Marshall McLuhan has even suggested that in the present age 'electric informational media' will complete displace the printed word; not only will there be no novels in the not so distant future but there will be no books of any kind. It is dangerously easy to be smug and say that in the twenty years or so that have elapsed since McLuhan disturbed us with his prophecies of the extinction of printed language the book-publishing industry has continued to flourish. The fact is that the media of film and television – especially the latter – have had a crucial effect on habits of perception, taste and the organization of leisure which has inevitably altered the attitude of many people to the reading of books, particularly books of fiction. Many publishers, too, have adopted new strategies for launching novels. They no longer hope for the manuscript of a splendid, original new work to arrive in the mail: they will negotiate with authors and their agents and will quite often pay large sums of money for the rights of a work which has not yet been written if it seems likely that the book, when completed, will appeal to a vast readership and be suitable for adaptation to the small or large screen or both. Nevertheless, seriously conceived novels are still written in quite large numbers and are still published.

The novel offers an experience quite different from that which we receive from watching a film or play. The reading of a novel is far more of a collaboration between reader and author; the pages of print have to be translated into images; the reader must exercise his imagination to bring the characters and events to life. The screen presents the things themselves, the men and women, the landscape, the flora and fauna: the image-making faculty of the audience is simply not required. Watching a play, whether on the stage or screen, is an essentially passive experience. However deeply we may be moved we are not involved *creatively* as we are when we read a good novel. If McLuhan's prophecy were to be fulfilled, if we were no longer able to respond to written fiction, there would be a real danger that our imagination, the power to invent, to enter the consciousness of people quite different from ourselves, would atrophy, with the consequence that humanity itself would be reduced. The novel is a powerful weapon in the struggle against mankind becoming automatized in an increasingly technological world and we should be grateful that it is still in good health.

I do not think that my assertion of the novel's robustness is a matter of wishful thinking and evidence of that health may be seen in the great breadth of its range both in Britain and America. In Britain the influence of the modernist movement, that pervasive mood of experimentation which was so strong in the twenties and thirties, has been quietly and selectively absorbed: the stream of consciousness technique of interior monologue and dialogue has been employed in works which are, in other respects, traditional fictional structures. The work of D. H. Lawrence, which was not experimental in the sense that the writings of Joyce and Woolf were, has been at least partially an inspiraton to a new regionalism found in the novels of David Storey, Melvyn

Bragg and a newcomer as a novelist though well-known as a
poet, Glyn Hughes. At present Storey is probably the most
impressive of these, though this tentative judgement is not
intended either to be conclusive or to minimize the achievement of the others.

David Storey

David Storey was born in Yorkshire in 1933, the son of a
miner. He won a scholarship to the Slade School of Art, and
while still a student there, he would travel back to the West
Riding each weekend to play professional Rugby League foot-
ball. His first novel, *This Sporting Life* (1960), drew upon his
first-hand experience as a professional athlete. Its central
character is Machin, a northern Rugby League footballer, a
man of limited intelligence but great physical strength, and
the book explores his inarticulate love for his widowed landlady and his blind urge towards courses of action which can
end only in self-destruction. *This Sporting Life* is a remarkable
study of working-class life in the North, its puritanism, moral
inflexibility, guilt and violence.

Storey went on to write successful plays as well as
further novels and in 1976 he published his most ambitious
work to date, *Saville*, a long, partly autobiographical novel
which is clearly in the Dickensian (through D. H. Lawrence)
mode, with darkly Lawrentian excursions into the psychology
of family relationships. It is set in a South Yorkshire mining
village and it begins with the birth of Saville's first child,
Andrew, in the late 1930s. Seville, a coal-miner, and his wife,
Ellen, adore their first child whose death, at the age of five, is
described with a restraint and simplicity which is poignantly
effective. Ellen is three months pregnant at the time of
Andrew's death and her next child, Colin, is the central character of the book. Although the novel is written in the third
person most of the events and people are seen through Colin's
eyes and Storey is successful in presenting both an objective
account of a particular social milieu at a particular time,
almost a compressed history of northern working-class life in
the period covering the Second World War and extending to

David Storey   the 1960s, and an exploraton of the development of his pro-
tagonist and his relationships inside and outside the family.

Saville proves that the traditional methods of unfolding a narrative, when supported by acuteness of observation
and a firm refusal to falsify the truth, may still result in a work
of literature that is both highly readable and capable of dealing with problems of living and loving which are timeless.
There is a quality in Storey's prose that is related to the landscape he describes so well: his language is plain, put together
in solid, workmanlike fashion. He avoids abstractions and
does not attempt the delicate, filigree effects that more lyrical
or subtle writers strive for. His is not the only way for a novelist to write, but it is the right way for what he has to say, and I
think few readers will fail to enjoy it.

anti-modernism

The other no-nonsense anti-modernist tradition, which probably stems from Fielding, through Dickens, Bennett and
Wells, is to be found first in the picaresque comic novels of the
fifties and sixties, the best-known and prototypical being
Kingsley Amis's Lucky Jim (1954), and, second, in the more
serious studies of provincial life – often working or lower
middle class – of Alan Sillitoe, Stan Barstow and John Wain. A
parallel middle- or upper-class fiction, less bluntly masculine
though not necessarily written by women, descending from
Jane Austen, George Eliot and Henry James, continues to
appear and, in the hands of such novelists as Angus Wilson,
A. S. Byatt and Iris Murdoch has proved to be vigorously and
satisfyingly alive, though the realism of each of these writers
is spiced by elements of the mythic or fabulous.

Iris Murdoch (b. 1919) has adopted the traditional
apparatus of plot, careful description of locale and character,
but she introduces into her stories elements of fantasy and
intellectual game-playing which belong to another and more
recent mode and the brilliance of her later novels, especially
The Black Prince (1973), The Sacred and Profane Love
Machine (1974) and A Word Child (1975) would have
delighted Nabokov, with whom she has something in

common. What they share is an excitement over the patterning
of events and the interplay of character and symbol to create a
completely realized fictional world. Both Nabokov and
Murdoch can be read for the simple pleasure of the story but
both are offering the reader more than this primary and necessary element. Each is also concerned with making a statement
about human existence which the story will enact; the small
local truths discovered by the plot will point to an embracing
local truth which can only be apprehended through the exercise of the imagination. Where they differ is in their attitudes
to style: for Nabokov the manipulation of language is so
exciting that he can be diverted from his main business as a
novelist by the exuberance of his verbal games, by the
temptation to dazzle us with his verbal pyrotechnics. Murdoch
writes well, often eloquently, but for her words are primarily
functional; they are there to embody important ideas, to
delineate character, to further the machinations of plot.

John Updike

The American, John Updike (b. 1932), is closer to Nabokov in
his relish for the phonetic and chromatic possibilities of
language employed in the construction of realistic narrative
which carries strong symbolic or mythic overtones. He is one
of the most entertaining novelists writing in the English
language today: his work shows an acute intelligence,
psychological subtlety and depth, a wonderful comic sense
and a profound sympathy with human frailty and aspiration.
Partly because of the sheer fluency and apparent
effortlessness of his prose style he has been seriously
underrated by some of those critics who are inclined to
mistake bulk and undisciplined energy for strength. Leslie A.
Fiedler, in his 'Study of the American literary scene from
Hemingway to Baldwin', *Waiting for the End* (1964), dismisses
Updike as '. . .that *New Yorker* writer much touted recently by
those who want the illusion of vision and fantasy without
surrendering the kind of reassurance provided by slick
writing at its most professionally *all right.*' It is true that this

judgement was formed early in Updike's career, but even by the early sixties it should have been evident that he was a writer of remarkable gifts.

In 1960 he published his second novel, *Rabbit, Run*, which was to be followed – though with other novels and collections of stories intervening – by two more books dealing with the same central character, Harry Angstrom. In *Rabbit, Run* we meet the young Angstrom, a former star of the basketball court, who is now married with a three-year-old son and a pregnant wife, and condemned to a suburban life of conventional domestic routine. He is tormented by a sense of loss, the baffled feeling that there must be something more to life than this slow, inexorable leaking away of what was once fresh, vigorous, illimitable. The suburban environment, evoked with precision and power, seems to be an elaborate, ever-tightening trap from which the only escape will be the indifference of exhaustion, senescence and, finally, death. The instinct to escape is strong, so strong indeed that Angstrom obeys it without the least idea of where to escape to. He simply runs away. Briefly he finds sanctuary in the arms and bed of Ruth but he leaves her – also pregnant – to return to his wife, Janice, who has by now been delivered of a baby daughter who is drowned when Janice, in an alcoholic daze, is trying to bath her. A bleak enough story of urban frustration, anxiety and despair, but it is not in the least depressing because Updike's beautifully supple prose, his sharp and steady eye for nuances of speech and gesture and his unsentimental but profound concern for every character result in a work which contains much of the comedy, pathos and momentary ecstasies of life itself.

Angstrom's story is next taken up in *Rabbit Redux* (1971) when Harry, ten years older but not perceptibly any wiser, has been re-united with Janice, but she turns the tables on her husband by deserting him for a smooth Greek car salesman employed by her father's company, Springer Motors. Harry becomes involved with two wild young non-conformists, Skeeter and Jill, who together and separately bring him to the very edge of doom. But he is, above all, a survivor and in *Rabbit is Rich* (1982) we find him established as boss of Springer Motors (left to him by his father-in-law) and enjoying – though 'enjoying' is perhaps too vigorous a word for his narrowly cosy existence – modest affluence. His son, Nelson, is grappling with, or rather wriggling among, similar problems to those which Harry fled from in his own young manhood, and the father has little to offer the son in the way of practical advice or consolation.

Rabbit is Rich has received less than whole-hearted praise. Some critics have found Angstrom's apparent acceptance of age and mortality too negative, reflecting a pessimistic view of life, unrelieved by expectations of anything which might illumine the gathering shades. But the elegance of phrasing, wit and observation are unimpaired and there is a kind of defiance in Angstrom's refusal to accept absolutely the limits placed on possibility by circumstance. One feels – though Updike does not state it explicitly – that Rabbit might yet take flight again and that his running might prove to be not merely away from the insupportable but towards a goal of at least partial enlightenment, for the 'Rabbit' novels, despite their irony, comedy and erotic preoccupations, are in a cautious, almost furtive way, religious in their unease, in the feeling experienced by Harry Angstrom that there exists 'the thing behind everything', some concealed coherence behind the blind disorder and fragmentation of modern life.

James Purdy

Another American novelist of a slightly older generation who shows some of the Nabokovian fascination with the novel's structure and delight in verbal pyrotechnics is James Purdy (b. 1932), whose most impressive novel, *Cabot Wright Begins* (1965) concerns itself, but in a more fantastic manner, with the same problems which Updike explores in the 'Rabbit' sequence. Cabot Wright is a Wall Street executive, educated at Yale, a man who would be considered by many, perhaps most people, to be enviably successful. But he is not content. He become a rapist, not through lust or hatred or vengeance but through sheer boredom. Life has become monochrome, intolerably tedious and only through gratuitous acts of outrageous violence can he find release from that stifling greyness. Again we find another version of the American

John Updike

James Purdy

novelist's view of the quest for identity, the struggle against the extinction of individuality constantly threatened by technological developments, media-manipulation and the spreading infection of boredom.

Cabot Wright Begins is very much aware of its own nature as a novel and Purdy slyly introduces references to the state of American fiction into the events and dialogue of his story. Cabot Wright is caught and imprisoned for his criminal activities and, shortly after his release, a character called Bernie Gladhart is persuaded by his wife Carrie to go to New York to find the rapist and write his life-story. When Bernie voices his doubts about his own qualifications to write the story Carrie tells him that all he has to do is '. . .write the truth like fiction'. This comment or counsel is an ironic reference to the practice, started by Truman Capote (b. 1925) with *In Cold Blood* (1966), of producing what have come to be known as non-fiction novels, stories in which the events and characters are drawn from actuality but are presented in the forms we associate with the novel.

non-fiction novels

The non-fiction novel is reportage in that it supplies facts, but it is dramatized by the kind of descriptive writing and use of dialogue not customarily used by journalists.

This heightened journalism, though enjoyable and sometimes, as in the hands of a writer of Capote's ability, illuminating, can neither claim to be a new kind of novel nor can it replace the more traditional kind of fiction. Apart from pure fantasy all fiction has its roots in reality: one of the great differences between the popular 'commercial' novel and the serious work of the imagination is that in the first, however packed with factual detail – brand-names, accurate information about firearms, diet, flight schedules, police procedures and so on – the characters are usually based, not on living, unpredictable, contradictory humans but on the stereotypes of similar fictions or television and cinema, while the characters in the best novels are people who can surprise us and awake in us real love, anxiety, admiration, disappointment and dislike. In

E. L. Doctorow's *Ragtime* (1975) historical figures such as the
multi-millionaire financiers J. P. Morgan and Henry Ford, and
the escapologist, Houdini, appear, not simply in walking-on
parts to give verisimilitude to the evocation of period and
background, but as fully realized characters, but this device is
new only in that the personages are taken from the very
recent past. Historical novelists have been using eminent
figures of the period in which their works are set for the past
two hundred years.

self-consciousness of the novelist

What is new in much of the fiction of the past twenty years is
the self-consciousness of the novelist as artist or fabricator, a
self-consciousness which permits itself overt expression in
novels like John Fowles's *The French Lieutenant's Woman*
(1969) in which pastiche – that is the imitation of earlier
fictional modes – is deliberately used to investigate the relationships between literary conventions, and social and
psychological realities.

    The French Lieutenant's Woman is, at its first level, a
romantic love story set in the second half of the nineteenth
century, written in the form and style of the best fiction of that
period. Until we reach the 13th chapter we could almost be
reading a Victorian novel, but at this point the author steps, as
it were, out of the wings and breaks the narrative spell with
these words: 'The story I am telling is all imagination. These
characters I create never existed outside my own mind. If I
have pretended until now to know my characters' minds and
innermost thought it is because I am writing in (just as I have
assumed some of the vocabulary and 'voice of') a convention
universally accepted at the time of my story: that the novelist
stands next to God. . .' He then goes on to suggest alternative
ways of ending his novel.

    To the attentive reader this manoeuvre is less startling
than one might expect because Fowles has previously
indicated in various ways that he is doing something other
than writing a pastiche of the Victorian romantic novel. Each
chapter is headed by a quotation which refers either to

Darwin or Marx or to the most popular and characteristic poetry of the age – that of Hardy, Clough, Arnold and Tennyson, all of whom were preoccupied by the religious problems presented by scientific rationalism – and there are passages in the body of the novel where Fowles not only makes references to the fiction of Dickens, Jane Austen and Hardy but imitates their styles. The result is a book which is intended to work upon the reader at different levels: it is first to be enjoyed as a romantic fiction, then as a commentary on the novelist's art, its scope and limitations; it examines that period in modern history – the second half of the nineteenth century – when the consciousness of Western man experienced a radical change, when the solid rock on which his deepest beliefs were based was suddenly shown to be as flimsy as a cardboard stage-prop.

Fowles is a resourceful writer with a strong gift for pure narrative but in *The French Lieutenant's Woman* he seems perversely determined to sabotage his own major strength. There are subtler ways of writing novels which are meant to function, self-consciously, on other levels than the elementary one of presenting imaginary people and events as if they were historical realities. Iris Murdoch, for example, possesses a story-telling facility which is every bit as compelling as that of Fowles but she is also capable of weaving philosophical and aesthetic explorations into the narrative fabric without disturbing its pattern. In other words we can read a Murdoch novel simply as an engrossing tale: the moral, psychological or philosophical commentary is there as a bonus for the reader who wishes to explore below the surface. *The Black Prince* (1973), for instance, is a highly readable tragi-comic account of an ageing novelist's love for the young daughter of a fellow-author. But it is also a complex study of the relationship of art to life, of truth to lies, of fiction to fact.

women novelists

The remarkable flowering of talent among women novelists which has been a feature of English fiction since the end of the Second World War has included a number of writers of great

intellectual sophistication who, like Iris Murdoch, use their art
for purposes beyond simple entertainment, novelists of the
quality of Doris Lessing, Penelope Mortimer, Muriel Spark,
Margaret Drabble, A. S. Byatt and Beryl Bainbridge. All of
these authors have produced work which is both popular and
of high artistic merit; however, I should like to draw the
attention here to two women novelists whose remarkable gifts
have not yet received the kind of critical approval which has
been granted to the writers mentioned above. This may be
because these two are not self-consciously 'experimental' in
their writings: each in her different way is content to work
within the tradition of the realistic novel though both are able
to develop within that tradition disturbing metaphoric and
poetic visions of the world we inhabit.

Elizabeth Taylor

Elizabeth Taylor (1912–1975) is one of the most accomplished
and enjoyable novelists of the past three decades. On the
surface her books deal with the problems of the English
middle classes, especially the female middle classes, marriage,
bereavement, coming to terms with growing old, understanding the young, falling in love, but below these concerns move
shapes of menace, anxiety, the unpredictable and terrifying.
Her prose is supremely economic and its rhythms possess a
delicate steeliness. She is capable of lyricism, wit and high
drama. Her last novel, *Blaming* (1976), begins with a middle-
aged English couple, Nick and Amy Henderson, on holiday in
Istanbul. Nick is a painter who is convalescing after a recent
illness. He and Amy make the acquaintance of an American
novelist, a young woman called Martha who is travelling alone
on the same tour. Nick, with quite unexpected suddenness, dies
and Martha assumes responsibility for the grief-stricken Amy
and accompanies her back to England. The rest of the novel, in
which many other vividly realized characters are introduced, is
a perceptive and profoundly original analysis of the ambivalent
relationship that develops between Amy and Martha and, as in
life, the reader finds it necessary to revise many earlier impressions of character and situation as events proceed.

Jennifer Johnston

The ability to create characters who gradually reveal un-expected facets of personality and temperament as the action unfolds, who possess the power both to surprise and convince us of their reality, is exhibited in all of Elizabeth Taylor's novels and is a gift possessed, too, by Jennifer Johnston (b. 1930), whose most remarkable work to date is *How Many Miles to Babylon?* (1974). This short novel is an astounding imaginative achievement. It is written in the first person and the central character is a young, upper-class Irishman, Alexander, an officer in the British Army during the First World War. We witness in flashback his childhood in the big house outside Dublin and his growing friendship with Jerry, a peasant boy, a relationship which is strongly disapproved of by Alexander's appalling mother. When war breaks out Alexander, at the insistence of his mother, joins the army and finds that Jerry is a private soldier in the same unit which is sent out to France. Just as, earlier, the snobbishness of Alexander's mother forbade his friendship with Jerry, so in the trenches it is forbidden by the rigid hierarchial military caste-system. Jerry receives a letter from his mother which, in its scarcely literate way, tells him that his father, who is also serving in the British Army, has been reported missing, and the young Irish peasant sets off on a hopeless search in no-man's land for the body, dead or alive, of the missing soldier. He is regarded by the authorities as having deserted and, on his return, he is placed under arrest, court-martialled and sentenced to death. Alexander is to command the firing squad.

The tragic resolution of events is handled with great tact and is both deeply moving and entirely convincing. The other characters – Alexander's brother-officer, Bennett, his commanding officer, Glendinning, and his dreadful mother and sad, defeated father – are portrayed with deft and sharp-eyed accuracy. Jennifer Johnston's handling of dialogue reveals a faultless ear for the rhythms and inflections of natural speech, and the evocations of landscape and of physical action are beautifully achieved. *How Many Miles to Babylon?* is a small masterpiece.

American women novelists

If there does not seem to have been a similar efflorescence of female talent among novelists in the United States this is probably because there was no scarcity of major American women writers in the first half of the twentieth century. Where, in Britain, we could boast only of Virginia Woolf and perhaps Ivy Compton-Burnett, America had produced many female authors of comparable stature including Edith Wharton, Willa Cather, Eudora Welty, Carson McCullers, Flannery O'Connor and Mary McCarthy. However, there are two American women novelists who, in their very different ways, have shown exceptional talent in work produced during the past twenty years: these are Joyce Carol Oates (b. 1938) and Alison Lurie (b. 1926).

Joyce Carol Oates

Joyce Carol Oates is a writer in the powerful, mythic tradition of which William Faulkner is the greatest exponent. She is an immensely prolific author and her sheer imaginative energy and the richness and variety of her invention, accompanied by a vigorous and colourful prose-style, equip her more than adequately to continue that tradition. Her novel *Angel of Light* (1982) explores the topical themes of power, politics and urban guerilla activities in Washington DC but the story is given a haunting universality by the narrative parallels with Greek tragedy. A wife and mother, like Clytemnestra, betrays and destroys her husband who is later avenged by his son and daughter. Joyce Carol Oates demonstrates, dramatically and convincingly, the ways in which power corrupts and, behind the opulence and apparently civilized veneer of Washington society, we see the primitive focus of greed, lust and envy victorious over moral honesty and idealism. One of the few honourable and idealistic characters is drowned in a swamp which exudes '...the rich black stink of decay' and the symbolism of this requires no underlining.

Alison Lurie

Alison Lurie, too, is much concerned with corruption and disillusionment in contemporary American society, but her
novels are closer in strategy and tone to the urbane tradition
of Mary McCarthy's *Groves of Academe* (1952) and *A
Charmed Life* (1955). *The War Between the Tates* (1974) is a
characteristic Lurie novel, arguably her most satisfying so far.
In this novel she explores the disintegration of a middle-class
American marriage with clinical precision and wit which does
not preclude an unsentimental compassion for the human
pain which is a real presence in this novel. Her principal characters are solidly created and their behaviour contains that
contradictoriness and inconsequentiality which persuades us
of their reality as living creatures.

Brian Tate and his wife, Erica, have two children, a
boy and a girl of fifteen and thirteen. The children have lost
their infant charm and they are both in their different but
equally abrasive ways asserting their independence. Brian,
who is a university teacher, has a hectic and messy affair with
Wendy, one of his students, and the novel traces the dissolution of the marriage which follows Erica's discovery of her
husband's infidelity. The enclosed campus society with its
feuds, gossip, political manoeuvering and ideological conflicts
mirrors the larger social confusion of the outside world, the
world of President Nixon, political chicanery, moral instability
and international fear and unrest. The novel is funny and
touching and unflinchingly honest in its confrontation with
the inadequacies of the principal characters and the system in
which they are trapped. No easy solution is offered to the
problems posed. Love is the only effective solvent yet, in some
of its guises, it seems at least as destructive as hatred and fear.

the 'campus novel'

The 'campus novel', of which Mary McCarthy's *The Groves of
Academe* was a stylish and original early example, continued
to flourish in the sixties and seventies from the pens of both
male and female writers in America. Perhaps because

American novelists are now very often associated with universities either as professors or 'writers in residence', in a way that very few British writers are, there is a profusion of novels dealing with academic life in the United States and a scarcity of such works from English novelists. However David Lodge in *Changing Places* (1975) and Malcolm Bradbury in *Stepping Westward* (1965) found in the idea of British and American writers or academics exchanging their environments a fruitful source of satire, comedy and social comment. *Stepping Westward*, apart from being a delightful comic novel, is especially interesting for the way in which, implicitly, a point about European and American culture is made. The period when, as in Henry James's novels, the American in search of artistic and intellectual nourishment was compelled to visit the great cities of Europe – Rome, Paris, London, places in which he wandered, wide-eyed and humbled by the riches of the past, an innocent abroad – has passed. It is the European now who is the innocent traveller bewildered by the vitality and opulence, both material and intellectual of the New World.

the 'campus novel'

In the foregoing pages I have done no more than name a few of the authors and their novels of the past two decades or so which appeal especially to my taste and which, I believe, will offer enjoyment to many readers. A full survey of the best fiction of this period would require the space of at least one large volume but I hope that I have scattered enough tempting pointers in the form of authors' names and titles of books to encourage readers to explore for themselves the rich and varied territory of recent novels in the English language. I am well aware of the vast number of excellent novelists who have not received so much as a passing reference – writers of the sterling quality of James Kennaway, William Trevor, Piers Paul Read, Paul Theroux, Brian Moore and Martin Amis – but I feel sure that anyone who reads and enjoys contemporary fiction will soon find his way to the writers who will most satisfyingly fulfil his imaginative and emotional needs.

Again limitation of space has precluded reference to categories of fiction such as the popular 'romances', science fiction, crime novels, Western and 'whodunnits'. I find here less cause for regret since there is little that one can profitably say about these beyond suggesting certain authors and titles for the addict to obtain. This is not, of course, to say that, roughly within these categories, we may not find works of real literary distinction. The best crimes novels of Dashiell Hammett and Raymond Chandler are works which apprentice novelists with more 'serious' aspirations might study with considerable benefit, and science-fiction has attracted the talents of distinguished writers on both sides of the Atlantic. Nevertheless I feel justified in concentrating on the work of those novelists who do not confine themselves to the categories of popular fiction, most of which is written to be read once only with no more serious purpose than to occupy a few idle hours, to provide an escape from, not a penetration into, reality.

The first meeting with the work of an author whom you have never before read can be as stimulating and rewarding as a new and congenial friendship, and the proper reading of a good novel, involving as it does your imaginative sympathy, questioning intelligence and moral judgement, is an experience which is not only intensely pleasurable but of lasting value. I believe that what we read is not only an indication of what we are: it can actually and fundamentally change us. The man or woman who does not read novels at all is usually deficient in imagination and in a sensitive response to experience; those who read only third-rate escapist fiction will exhibit predictable and dull attitudes to life: The reader of excellent fiction will be rewarded by deep enjoyment and by insights into the mysteries of human existence to which he would otherwise be blind. So let us explore.

9

EXPLORING FICTION

Suppose you have read few, or even no, novels for a long time, perhaps since school-days, and now you wish to discover, or rediscover, the pleasures and rewards offered by the best fiction. The sheer quantity of available novels may well be confusing, even intimidating, so here are a few hints about ways in which to begin the exploration of fiction in the English language.

where to begin?

For a full and discerning appreciation of the literature of our own time it is necessary to possess a knowledge of the literature of the past but I do not believe that the novice-reader should necessarily begin his explorations on a sequential, chronological basis. Since novels are usually concerned with issues and problems of the times in which they are written – and this, paradoxically, could be as true of the historical novel or science-fiction fantasy as of an overtly topical work – it follows that our interest will be more easily engaged by stories dealing with the contemporary world than with a past time of which we may be largely ignorant though, of course, the greatest work transcends its time and place and contains universal, timeless truths. Nevertheless most readers will find that a modern novel will probably be more easily and agreeably assimilable than, say, a heavyweight, epistolary novel of the eighteenth century, and the novel you choose should be one which does not require a literary sophistication you do not feel you possess. In other words, only the exceptional reader who begins his journey with James Joyce's *Ulysses* or – Heaven forbid – *Finnegan's Wake* is likely to get beyond a few pages.

This reference to Joyce, who is unquestionably one of the greatest prose writers of this or any other century, brings me to an important truth and one which is often obscured by teachers and academic critics. It is this: every one of us is in some way limited by his or her individual predilections, needs, education, intellectual and emotional resources, prejudices, environment, personal psychology and so on. There are bound to be masterpieces of literature to which we are blind and deaf however hard we try to respond to them. I am convinced that each of us has at least one blind-spot in this sense. So if you find that a certain novel which has been held up as a magnificient work of genius which will bring you ineffable delight and illumination is in fact virtually meaningless, or just plain boring, do not feel either that you have failed or that those who have praised the book are liars. It is simply that this book does not answer your particular needs. The world of fiction is vast and varied: you will find the masterpiece that does indeed address you personally, so personally indeed that you will feel that its author wrote it for you alone. And where will this work be found? Almost certainly, I think, in a public library.

public libraries

The public libraries in Great Britain are among the glories of our state. Naturally they vary in size and in efficiency but almost every town of any size has a library service which is at least useful and frequently excellent, and all of the larger cities are furnished with splendid central libraries with their smaller suburban satellites. Even the smallest – the rural mobiles for instance – will always be prepared to obtain specified books on request and a competent librarian is usually on hand to supply information about authors and their works. You will find the alphabetically arranged fiction section perfectly easy to explore provided you know the name of the author you are looking for. If, on the other hand, you wish to be more adventurous and try to make some unaided discoveries among contemporary fiction, it is easy to get an idea of which publishers are likely to produce the work of interesting new writers.

public libraries

new novels

Most general publishers do include on their lists a certain number of new novels each publishing season. Firms such as Chatto and Windus, Secker and Warburg, Faber and Faber, Jonathan Cape, the Bodley Head, Longmans and Hodder and Stoughton, to mention only a few, are unlikely to publish inferior fiction. A novel bearing the imprint of any one of these firms is virtually certain to possess some literary merit, so it is a good idea to make a note of not only the author but the publisher of any book which you happen upon and find enjoyable, the chances being that other works published by the same firm will prove to be to your taste. But this 'blindfold' reaching out to the bookshelves in the hope of making rewarding discoveries is less likely to provide satisfaction than an informed selectivity, and to keep abreast of the most interesting work being written by contemporary novelists it will be necessary to read the best literary journalism available.

new novels

reading reviews

All of the serious daily and weekly newspapers print reviews of the new fiction. Among the dailies the *Guardian, The Times*

reading reviews

and *The Daily Telegraph* give more space and serious attention to new books than the more popular press, but the most
thorough and informed criticism of fiction is to be found in the
specialist weekly or monthly literary journals such as the
Times Literary Supplement, and the *London Review of Books.*
New fiction is also reviewed regularly and competently in the
Sunday newspapers, *The Observer, The Sunday Times* and
The Sunday Telegraph. The weekly trade journal of the publishing industry, the *Bookseller,* contains details of all new
books, including novels, and it is subscribed to by all book
retailers and libraries. If you regularly read the literary pages
of your daily and weekly newspaper and compare the critical
assessments of novels appearing in, say, the *Guardian, The
Sunday Times* and *The Times Literary Supplement* you will at
least learn who the promising new authors are and which
books are generally reckoned to be the ones worth reading.
Not all reviewers will be in agreement over the merits of a
recently published novel, but you should be able to tell from
their comments whether or not the book is worth your reading
so that you can form your own opinion. And here I should like
to make a useful practical suggestion. Keep a notebook – one
of those cheap little cash or memo books will serve the
purpose – and jot down the names of the author and publisher
of any book which seems, from the notices you have read or
from personal recommendation, likely to be of interest. This
notebook should prove a valuble prompter on your visits to
the library when you may wish to look for, or order, a
particular novel.

radio book programmes

There are, of course, other sources of information about new
fiction than those provided by the book-pages of the daily or
weekly press. BBC radio transmits a number of programmes
in which new novels are reviewed or old ones read serially or
adapted for dramatic broadcasting. Radio 3's *Critics' Forum,* a
weekly survey of the arts, always includes a book for discussion, though novels have to take their turn with other kinds of
literature. *Kaleidoscope,* the Radio 4 arts programme which is

broadcast on five nights each week, will sometimes choose a work of fiction to be reviewed and *Bookshelf,* the only programme devoted to books – a niggardly half-hour per week – also periodically deals with novels, either of the past or present, but rarely in a more than superficial way. The novel is served better, I think, by the usually skilful serial readings such as *A Book at Bedtime* and *Story Time* and in the excellent dramatizations which are broadcast from time to time.

television adaptations

Television, too, has produced some fine adaptations of novels that seem to send viewers to the printed pages of the books from which the dramatizations have been taken: Dickens, Trollope, Evelyn Waugh and Jennifer Johnston are a few of the novelists whose work has been successfully adapted for the small screen. The serious discussion of fiction or any other kind of literature on television is a rare event. Every now and then the BBC's *Omnibus* or ITV's *The South Bank Show* will feature an interview with a novelist but, interesting though such programmes may be, they add little to our knowledge of the mysterious power of literature. Evelyn Waugh, Iris Murdoch, Saul Bellow, John Updike and many other eminent novelists have made personal appearances on our screens but, however amusing and informative they may have been, it is only in the reading of their books that we are given direct access to their genius.

building your library

Among the novels that you will read some, however gripping and enjoyable at the time, will not be among the comparatively few books that you know you will wish to return to and read again, but will be borrowed from the library or from friends. However, there are novels, and a quite considerable number, which you will wish to keep on your shelves, and the acquisition of your own private library is a process which will

**building
your
library**

give great satisfaction. Nor need it be, despite the great increase in the price of new books during the past few years, a very costly business, for there are many ways of minimizing the expense.

Firstly, second-hand bookshops generally contain large stocks of fiction and it is usually possible to pick up well-printed and pleasingly bound copies of the great classics very cheaply indeed. Recent novels, too, in hard covers and in good condition, are rarely priced at more than half of their original cost and very frequently at a good deal less. Public libraries have periodical clearances of their shelves to make room for the constant influx of new books. A few years ago it was their practice to dispose of these old books by selling them cheaply to be pulped for recycling but in recent times it has become common for the libraries to hold sales of unwanted stock and on these occasions first-class fiction of both the past and present can be bought at absurdly low prices. Quite recently a friend of mine picked up at a public library sale copies of novels by Ford Madox Ford, Scott Fitzgerald, Iris Murdoch, Dickens, Defoe, Smollett and Jane Austen, all in good condition, for less than he would have to pay for a single new paperback.

book clubs

book clubs

Some readers might be tempted by those advertisements in the colour supplements and popular magazines which invite subscriptions to a book club, offering as bait a choice of three or four new books at what seems a give-away price. Although many readers find that book clubs provide an attractive service, I have always resisted these offers. Once you have enrolled you are obliged to buy a certain number of books each year from those selected for publication by the club. This means to some extent someone is choosing your reading for you and the titles picked are usually those of the latest popular commercial successes.

To buy new novels, in hardback, can admittedly be quite costly. But not always. The Heinemann/Octopus Library, for example, has issued a series of reprints which are

astonishingly good value. Each very large volume, splendidly
bound and printed on excellent paper, contains between four
and eight of a chosen author's best novels. You can obtain in
this form seven novels by D. H. Lawrence and five by E. M.
Forster, to mention only two of the eminent writers available
in the series, at an average cost of one pound or less per novel.
But even on first publication a novel priced at, say, between
six and nine pounds is not unreasonably expensive. A visit to
the theatre can cost as much, and more; many of us fairly
frequently will spend double or treble the price of a novel on a
meal for two, and a couple of evenings in the pub could
absorb the cost of a new book. Furthermore, judicious buying
of new novels by distinguished or promising authors can be, in
a small but not derisory way, a practical investment.

book clubs

collectable books

There exists a lively demand by collectors for modern first
editions; the popular idea that only very old books may be
valuable is quite false. A first edition of an early novel by
Evelyn Waugh, Anthony Powell, or Graham Greene, if it is in
good condition and the dust-wrapper has been carefully pre-
served (this is important), could be sold today at something
like a hundred times its original cost, and a James Joyce first
edition would be at least worth its weight in fivers. I am not, of
course, suggesting that you should be guided in your book-
buying by such mercenary considerations, but it is a pleasant
thought that a book which has given you great pleasure is not
only a permanent possession but it may well be steadily
appreciating in pecuniary value.

**collectable
books**

paperbacks

Finally, the reader who is collecting a library of good fiction
should not assume that paperbacks are disposable because of
either the ephemerality of content or the flimsiness of their
physical make-up. In fact the best paperback publishers produce well-printed and firmly bound books with very attractive

paperbacks

paperbacks covers and the range is enormous. Not only can we obtain the best recent fiction very soon after it has been published in hardback, but the great novels of the recent and more distant past are available in pleasing and durable format.

I hope that, in this book, I have been able to give the reader some idea of how to set about his own voyage of discovery in the endlessly fascinating and changing seas of great fiction. We are living in times in which most people have more leisure than ever before; alas, the unemployed may be said to have far too much. Reading in general, and the reading of the finest fiction in particular, is a way, arguably the best possible, of using that leisure, for it can provide not only incalculable pleasure but understanding, sympathy and wisdom. And it need cost nothing. I am painfully aware of the limitations of the survey I have presented: great authors and their works have been dealt with in a far too summary and superficial way; many fine writers have been mentioned only by name, or not at all. But a reading of this book should at least provide a starting-point and the more the reader explores the areas so roughly sketched out here the more he will find that he can exercise his own judgement and make those personal discoveries which provide such intense delight and illumination.

recommended further reading

Aspects of the Novel, E. M. Forster. Edward Arnold

City of Words: American fiction 1950–1970, Tony Tanner. Jonathan Cape

Collected Essays, Graham Greene. Bodley Head

The Contemporary English Novel, eds. Malcolm Bradbury and David Pulmer. Edward Arnold

The Craft of Fiction, Percy Lubbock (1946)

The English Novel, Walter Allen. Penguin

Fiction and the Reading Public, Q. D. Leavis. Chatto & Windus

The Great Tradition, F. R. Leavis. Chatto & Windus

Growth of the English Novel, Richard Church. Methuen

An Introduction to the English Novel (2 Volumes), Arnold Kettle. Hutchinson

D. H. Lawrence: Selected Literary Criticism, ed. Anthony Beard. Heinemann

The Liberal Imagination, Lionel Trilling. Secker & Warburg

The Living Novel, V. S. Pritchett. Chatto & Windus

Love and Death in the American Novel, Leslie A Fiedler. Jonathan Cape

recommended further reading

The Modern Novel, Paul West. Hutchinson

The Novel 1940–1950, Longman for the British Council. Longman

The Novel Today, Walter Allen. Longman

The Situation of the Novel, Bernard Bergonzi (1970)

Some Principles of Fiction, Robert Liddell. Jonathan Cape

index